EASTMAN SCHOOL OF MUSIC SERIES

HANDBOOK *of* CONDUCTING

EASTMAN SCHOOL OF MUSIC SERIES

BASIC PRINCIPLES OF THE TECHNIQUE OF 18TH AND 19TH CENTURY COMPOSITION
By Allen Irvine McHose

SIGHT-SINGING MANUAL   By Allen Irvine McHose & Ruth Northup Tibbs

THE CONTRAPUNTAL HARMONIC TECHNIQUE OF THE EIGHTEENTH CENTURY
By Allen Irvine McHose

KEYBOARD AND DICTATION MANUAL   By Allen Irvine McHose & Donald F. White

CHORALE COLLECTION   By Elvera Wonderlich

TEACHERS DICTATION MANUAL   By Allen Irvine McHose

DIRECT APPROACH TO COUNTERPOINT IN SIXTEENTH CENTURY STYLE
By Gustave Fredric Soderlund

EXAMPLES OF GREGORIAN CHANT AND WORKS BY ORLANDUS LASSUS,
GIOVANNI PIERLUIGI PALESTRINA, AND MARC ANTONIO INGEGNERI
By Gustave Fredric Soderlund

EXAMPLES ILLUSTRATING THE DEVELOPMENT OF MELODIC LINE AND CONTRAPUNTAL
STYLE FROM GREEK MELODY TO MOZART   By Gustave Fredric Soderlund

TEXT ON ORCHESTRATION   By Bernard C. Rogers

HANDBOOK OF CONDUCTING   By Karl Van Hoesen

EXAMPLES OF MUSIC BEFORE 1400   By Harold Gleason

METHOD OF ORGAN PLAYING   By Harold Gleason

A MODERN METHOD FOR THE DOUBLE BASS   By Nelson Watson

Handbook of

CONDUCTING

Karl D. Van Hoesen, M. A.

INSTRUCTOR IN MUSIC EDUCATION
EASTMAN SCHOOL OF MUSIC
UNIVERSITY OF ROCHESTER
SENIOR CONSULTANT IN MUSIC FOR THE
BOARD OF EDUCATION, ROCHESTER, N. Y.

REVISED EDITION

New York

APPLETON-CENTURY-CROFTS INC.

PRINTED IN THE UNITED STATES OF AMERICA

FOREWORD

In writing <u>Handbook of Conducting</u>, Karl VanHoesen has added another valuable contribution to his pedagogic writings. The author is not only a conductor of distinguished ability but is also a gifted teacher who has been particularly successful in applying the pedagogy of his subject to the field of public school music.

Handbook of Conducting is above all a practical work, devoting its attention directly to important technical problems, the solution of which is essential if a sound conducting technic is to be established. The book contains many excerpts from scores which illustrate specific difficulties. That these illustrations are drawn from contemporary as well as from classic literature adds greatly to the value of this excellent handbook.

HOWARD HANSON,
Director, Eastman School of Music.

PREFACE

The work presented here is an outgrowth of the writer's effort over a period of years to provide for his students at the Eastman School of Music definite ways and means of mastering the elementary fundamentals of baton technique. In devising the following material, the author has not been unmindful of the lessons in conducting he received in former years from Eugene Goossens. The basis of much which might be called the type or style of technique advocated here is derived directly from the teaching of Mr. Goossens. The author is deeply grateful for having had the privilege, both as player and pupil, of coming under the influence of his superb technique.

The immediate need for illustrative examples of contemporary American music was brought to the author's attention by Dr. Howard Hanson, Director of the Eastman School of Music. Those who have had the privilege of coming under his personal influence as an administrator and a teacher can realize best how potent and far-reaching that influence has been. I hope that some of the sound and thorough principles of music education for which he stands may have found expression in this work.

The writer also wishes to acknowledge his very large debt to Dr. William S. Larson of the Eastman School of Music whose valuable suggestions were responsible for many improvements in material and arrangement.

Mr. James M. Spinning has given many valuable suggestions which have resulted in making the manuscript more presentable. The author is grateful for his help.

Mr. Joseph Roeber, librarian of the Rochester Philharmonic Orchestra, has aided the author greatly in giving him access to original sources for musical examples. His help and suggestions are greatly appreciated.

Miss Eleanor Leek, Mr. George Yeager, and Mr. Maurice Foote have all contributed their services in helping to prepare the manuscript. Their capacities for taking pains in mechanical details have greatly enhanced whatever merit the book may have.

It is regretted that a more inspiring subject than the author could not have modeled for the photographs illustrating the various conducting gestures. Only clarity of illustration was sought. The writer is greatly indebted to Mr. Llyle Keith, of the Eastman School, for his painstaking care in making the photographs.

TABLE OF CONTENTS

Page

FOREWORD   v
PREFACE   vii
LIST OF DIAGRAMS   xiii
LIST OF ILLUSTRATIONS   xv
LIST OF MUSICAL EXAMPLES   xvii

Chapter

  I. INTRODUCTION   1
 II. THE TECHNIQUE OF CONDUCTING   4
      A. General Principles of Baton Manipulation   4
         1. The Preparatory or Cue-beat   4
         2. The Beat Recoil   5
         3. Spacial Extent and Character of Beats   5
III. THE PREPARATORY POSITION   6
 IV. THE TWO-BEAT MEASURE   9
      A. Mechanical Exercises on the Two-beat for the Development of
         Rhythmic Clarity and Style   9
  V. REASONS FOR FAULTY BEAT MANIPULATION WITH CORRECTIVE EXERCISES . .   11
 VI. METHOD OF PROCEDURE FOR THE STUDY OF MUSICAL EXAMPLES AND MUSICAL
      EXAMPLES FOR THE TWO-BEAT MEASURE   15
      A. Method of Procedure   15
      B. Musical Examples   15
VII. THE THREE-BEAT MEASURE   20
      A. Mechanical Exercises on the Three-beat for the Development of
         Rhythmic Clarity and Style   20
      B. Musical Examples   21
VIII. THE FOUR-BEAT MEASURE   26
      A. Rhythmic Exercises   26
      B. Musical Examples   27
 IX. THE FIVE-BEAT MEASURE   31
      A. Secondary Accent on Three   31
      B. Secondary Accent on Four   31
      C. Rhythmic Exercises   31
      D. Musical Examples   32
  X. THE SIX-BEAT MEASURE   35
      A. Rhythmic Exercises   35
      B. Musical Examples   36
 XI. THE SEVEN-BEAT MEASURE   38
      A. Secondary Accent on Four   38
      B. Secondary Accent on Five   38
      C. Secondary Accents on Three and Five   39
      D. Seven-beat as Uneven Two or Three   39
      E. Rhythmic Exercises   39
      F. Musical Examples   40

Chapter   Page

XII. THE EIGHT-BEAT MEASURE . . . 42
  A. Eight as Compound Four . . . 42
  B. Eight Without Subdivision . . . 42
  C. Rhythmic Exercises . . . 43
  D. Musical Examples . . . 43
XIII. THE NINE-BEAT MEASURE . . . 45
  A. Rhythmic Exercises . . . 45
  B. Musical Examples . . . 46
XIV. OTHER DIVIDED MEASURES . . . 47
  A. The Divided Two-beat . . . 47
  B. The Divided Three-beat . . . 47
  C. The Divided Six-beat . . . 48
  D. Rhythmic Exercises . . . 48
  E. Musical Examples . . . 48
XV. THE TEN- AND ELEVEN-BEAT MEASURES . . . 50
  A. Ten-eight in Four . . . 50
  B. Eleven-eight in Four . . . 50
  C. Ten as Divided Five . . . 51
  D. Eleven as Three Plus Three Plus Three Plus Two . . . 52
XVI. THE TWELVE-BEAT MEASURE . . . 53
  A. Rhythmic Exercises . . . 53
  B. Rhythmic Sequence Exercises to be Conducted from Memory . . . 53
  C. Musical Example . . . 54
XVII. THE ONE-BEAT MEASURE . . . 55
  A. Rhythmic Exercises . . . 56
  B. Musical Examples . . . 57
XVIII. THE LEFT HAND . . . 58
  A. Left Hand as Time-beating Agent . . . 58
  B. Left-Hand Exercises . . . 58
  C. Left Hand for Indicating Crescendo and Diminuendo . . . 59
  D. Left Hand for Indicating Subito Piano and Subito Forte . . . 62
  E. Musical Examples . . . 64
  F. Left Hand for Indicating Entrances . . . 65
  G. Other Left-Hand Uses . . . 65
XIX. THE ATTACK . . . 66
  A. The Attack on the Beat . . . 66
  B. The Attack after the Beat . . . 68
  C. The Attack after the Up-beat . . . 69
  D. The Attack for Sustained Holds . . . 69
XX. THE FERMATA AND RELEASE . . . 71
  A. Examples of Release . . . 71
  B. Combining the Release with the Preparation for the Next Beat . . . 72
XXI. THE RITARD AND ACCELERANDO . . . 75
  A. Exercises for the Development of a Smooth Technique in the Ritard and Accelerando . . . 75
XXII. THE ACCENT . . . 77
  A. Exercises for the Study of the Technique of the Accent . . . 77
    1. Accent on One . . . 77
    2. Accent on Two . . . 77
    3. Accent on Three . . . 78
    4. Accent on Four . . . 78
  B. Off-beat Accents . . . 78

Chapter   Page

XXIII. ADDITIONAL TECHNICAL EXERCISE MATERIAL 80
XXIV.   MUSICAL EXAMPLES FROM AMERICAN COMPOSITIONS 85
XXV.   THE PSYCHOLOGICAL ASPECTS OF CONDUCTING 94
        A. Suggestions for Rehearsal Routine 94
        B. On Conducting from Memory 95
XXVI.   CONCLUSION 97
        BIBLIOGRAPHY 99

LIST OF DIAGRAMS

Diagram   Page

1. The Two-beat 9
2. The Two-beat (Albert Coates) 13
3. The Three-beat 20
4. The Four-beat 26
5. The Five-beat with Secondary Accent on the Third Beat 31
6. The Five-beat with Secondary Accent on the Fourth Beat 31
7. The Five-beat (Merging of the First and Second Beats) 32
8. The Six-beat 35
9. The Six-beat 35
10. The Seven-beat with Secondary Accent Falling on the Fourth Beat . . 38
11. The Seven-beat with Secondary Accent Falling on the Fifth Beat . . . 38
12. The Seven-beat with Secondary Accents Falling on Three and Five . . 39
13. The Eight or Compound Four-beat 42
14. The Eight-beat Measure Without Subdividing the Beats 42
15. The Nine-beat 45
16. The Incorrect Nine-beat 45
17. The Divided Two-beat 47
18. The Divided Three-beat 47
19. The Divided Six-beat 48
20. The Ten-beat Measure as Divided Five 51
21. The Ten-beat Measure as Divided Five (Different Grouping) 51
22. The Eleven-beat Measure 52
23. The Twelve-beat Measure 53
24. Preparatory Exercises for the One-beat 55
25. Ritard from a One into a Three 56
26. The Three-beat (Left Hand) 59
27. The Four-beat (Left Hand) 59
28. The Six-beat (Left Hand) 59
29. The Nine-beat (Left Hand) 59
30. For Starting on the First Beat of a Measure 66
31. For Starting a Three-beat Measure on the Second Beat 66
32. For Starting a Four-beat Measure on the Second Beat 67
33. For Starting a Four-beat Measure on the Third Beat 67
34. For Starting any Measure on its Last Beat 67
35. For Starting a Six-beat Measure on the Fifth Beat 67
36. For Starting a Nine-beat Measure on its Seventh Beat 67
37. Example of Release 71
38. Example of Release 71
39. Example of Release 71
40. Example of Release 71
41. Method of Attack and Release 72
42. Combining the Release with Preparation for the Next Beat, the Hold
    on One 73
43. Combining the Release with Preparation for the Next Beat, the Hold
    on Two 73

xiii

Diagram   Page

    44.   Combining the Release with Preparation for the Next Beat, the Hold
            on Three   73
    45.   Combining the Release with Preparation for the Next Beat, the Hold
            on Four   73
    46.   The Ritard from a Two into a Six   75
    47.   The Accent on One   77
    48.   The Accent on Two   77
    49.   The Accent on Three   78
    50.   The Accent on Four   78

LIST OF ILLUSTRATIONS

Figure   Page

1. Correct Preparatory Position of the Hand   6

2. Incorrect Preparatory Hand Position Showing Exaggerated Bend of Wrist   6

3. Incorrect Preparatory Hand Position Showing Exaggerated Bend of Elbow   6

4. Correct Preparatory Position   7

5. Correct Preparatory Position   7

6. Incorrect Preparatory Position Showing Unauthoritative Curl of Little
   Finger   8

7. Incorrect Preparatory Position Showing Exaggerated Upward Bend of
   Wrist   8

8. Incorrect Preparatory Position Showing Exaggerated Angle Between Baton and Hand   8

9. Incorrect Dropping of the Wrist on the Down-beat   11

10. Corrective Exercise for the Dropping of the Wrist   11

11. Incorrect Turning of the Hand   13

12. Beginning of Crescendo   60

13. Climax of Crescendo   60

14. Beginning of Diminuendo   61

15. Close of Diminuendo   61

LIST OF MUSICAL EXAMPLES

Example   Page

1. War March of the Priests from "Athalia" - Mendelssohn 15
2. Rakoczy March - Berlioz 16
3. Overture to "The Flying Dutchman" - Wagner 16
4. Introduction to the Third Act of "Lohengrin" - Wagner 16
5. Morning from "Peer Gynt Suite No. 1" - Grieg 17
6. March - "The Stars and Stripes Forever" - Sousa 17
7. Shepherd's Dance from "Three Dances from Henry VIII" - German . . . 18
8. Country Dance from "Nell Gwynn" - German 18
9. Overture - "Die Entführung aus dem Serail" - Mozart 19
10. Overture - "Figaros Hochzeit" - Mozart 19
11. Symphony in B-minor - Schubert 21
12. Symphony in B-minor (First movement) - .Schubert 21
13. Overture to "Egmont" - Beethoven (Allegro) 22
14. Symphony No. 3 (First movement) - Beethoven 22
15. Poupée Valsante - Poldini 22
16. Anitra's Dance from "Peer Gynt Suite No. 1" - Grieg 23
17. Mignon Overture - Ambroise Thomas 23
18. Excerpt from "The Bat" - Strauss 24
19. Overture to "Tannhäuser" - Wagner 24
20. Symphony No. 3 - Mendelssohn 24
21. Largo from "Xerxes" - Handel 25
22. Overture to "Die Meistersinger" - Wagner 27
23. Finale from Symphony in E Minor (The New World) - Dvorak 27
24. Finale from Symphony No. 4 - Tschaikowsky 28
25. Finale from Symphony No. 1 - Brahms 28
26. Overture to "Euryanthe" - von Weber 28
27. Procession of the Holy Grail from "Parsifal" - Wagner 29
28. Excerpt from Overture to "Der Freischütz" - von Weber 29
29. Symphony No. 6, Third movement - Tschaikowsky 30
30. Excerpt from Overture to "Euryanthe" - von Weber 30
31. Allegro from Symphony No. 6 - Tschaikowsky 32
32. Mars, the Bringer of War from "The Planets" - Holst 33
33. Egyptienne from "Silhouettes" - Hadley 33
34. Excerpt from "Petrouchska" - Stravinsky 34
35. Calm as the Night - Bohm 36
36. Andante from Symphony in G Minor - Mozart 36
37. Prelude to "Liebestod" - Wagner 37
38. Excerpt from "Mignon" - Thomas 2 37
39. Exercise in $\frac{7}{8}$ 40
40. Excerpt from Symphony No. 2 - Randall Thompson 40
41. Excerpt from Symphony No. 1 - Randall Thompson 41
42. Motet - Psalm CVIII, O God, My Heart is Ready - George Henry Day . 41
43. Air - J. S. Bach 43
44. Symphony No. 2 - Schubert 44
45. Sorcerer's Apprentice - Dukas 46

Example   Page

46.   Afternoon of a Faun - Debussy   46
47.   Excerpt from Irish from "Silhouettes" - Hadley   48
48.   Symphony No. 6 - Haydn   49
49.   Ten-eight in Four   50
50.   Eleven-eight in Four   51
51.   Concerto for Two Violins - J. S. Bach   54
52.   Scherzo from "Midsummer Night's Dream" - Mendelssohn   57
53.   Furiant from "The Bartered Bride" - Smetana   57
54.   Scherzo from Symphony No. 6 - Beethoven   57
55.   Exercise for Crescendo and Diminuendo   60
56.   Exercise for Crescendo and Diminuendo Varying the Beats   61
57.   Exercise for the Development of Technique in Indicating the Subito
        Forte and Piano   62
58.   Exercises for the Development of Technique in Indicating the Subito
        Forte and Piano   63
59.   Exercise for the Development of Technique in Indicating the Subito
        and Piano   63
60.   Exercise for the Development of Technique in Indicating the Subito
        Forte and Piano   63
61.   Overture to "Rosamunde," (Zauberharfe) - Schubert   64
62.   Excerpt from Overture to "Rosamunde" (Zauberharfe) - Schubert . . .   64
63.   Excerpt from Overture to "Rosamunde" (Zauberharfe) - Schubert . . .   64
64.   Excerpt from Overture to "Egmont" - Beethoven   64
65.   Excerpt from "Ruy Blas" - Mendelssohn   68
66.   Don Juan - Strauss   68
67.   Excerpt from Overture to "Rosamunde" (Zauberharfe) - Schubert . . .   69
68.   Excerpt from "Oberon" - von Weber   69
69.   Overture to "Egmont" - Beethoven   70
70.   Overture to "The Magic Flute" - Mozart   72
71.   Overture to "The Magic Flute" - Mozart   72
72.   Combining Release and Preparation for the Next Beat; the Hold on One 73
73.   Combining Release and Preparation for the Next Beat; the Hold on Two 73
74.   Combining the Release and Preparation for the Next Beat; Hold on
        Three   73
75.   Combining the Release and Preparation for the Next Beat; Hold on
        Four   73
76.   Traurigkeit - J. S. Bach   73
77.   O Gott, du frommer Gott - J. S. Bach   74
78.   Alles ist an Gottes Segen - J. S. Bach   74
79.   Was frag' ich nach der Welt - J. S. Bach   74
80.   Nun Prieset Alle - J. S. Bach   74
81.   Exercise for the Accent on One   77
82.   Exercise for the Accent on Two   77
83.   Exercise for the Accent on Three   78
84.   Exercise for the Accent on Four   78
85.   Excerpt from "The Magic Flute" - Mozart   78
86.   Excerpt from the Scherzo of Symphony No. 3 - Beethoven   79
87.   Excerpt from Symphony No. 2 - Beethoven   79
      Additional Technical Exercise Material   80
88.   The Pleasure Dome of Kubla Khan - Chas. T. Griffes   85
89.   Excerpt from "Romantic" Symphony - Howard Hanson   86

Example   Page

90a. Excerpt from "Pan and the Priest" - Howard Hanson 87
90b. Excerpt from "Pan and the Priest" - Howard Hanson 87
91.   Excerpt from "Romantic" Symphony - Howard Hanson 88
92.   Excerpt from "Pan and the Priest" - Howard Hanson 89
93.   Excerpt from "Tam-o-Shanter" - George Chadwick 90
94.   Excerpt from "Prarie", A Poem for Orchestra - Sowerby 91
95.   Excerpt from "Prarie" - Sowerby 91
96.   Excerpt from Concerto for Oboe - Irvine McHose 92
97.   Excerpt from "Three Eastern Dances" - Bernard Rogers 93

Chapter I

INTRODUCTION

To the average lay person, the time-beating function of the conductor is
most apparent. To music students who have been competently conducted in choral
singing or in orchestral playing, other phases of conducting may seem of greater
importance. Conducting is really a many-sided art. The mastery of its technique
is only a small part of the student's task. Even the sum total of technical
knowledge and skill, musical talent of the highest order, an exhaustive knowledge
of music, and years of experience in conducting and in being conducted may not be
sufficient equipment to assure success. The successful conductor must have all
of the intangible qualities of personality which are essential for forceful leadership. When many personalities with different emotional characteristics and
intellectual capacities are to be merged into one playing or singing unit which
must be subjected to the dominating personality of the conductor, this person
must possess a certain force of character. The technique of conducting can be
learned providing innate musicality and a certain motor capacity for rhythmic
precision are present. Knowledge and experience can be gained by perseverance.
The awareness of personal efficacy may become more and more apparent as opportun-
ity is offered to the serious student to exercise his talent and knowledge. The
suggestions in the following pages are designed to help in this development, but
no course of study can make a good conductor out of a poor musician, nor a forceful leader out of a weak personality. The ability of the potential conductor, to
whom these pages are addressed, therefore, will eventually be measured by many
factors which a course of study cannot include. On the ground that technical
proficiency is only one of the conductor's prerequisites, however, the feasibil-
ity of the attempt to codify rules and to assemble exercise and study material
need not be questioned. Technical skill must be acquired in order to clear the
way for musical expression. In devising material for this purpose, the author
has not been unmindful of the fact that nearly all competent conductors differ
in many phases of their art,--in matters of style in gesture, and in ideas of
tempo and interpretation. It is not necessary, because of this, to conclude
that there are not right and wrong ways of conducting. Different types of technique may be employed to achieve good results, but poor, ragged, and unbalanced
musical performances always result from clumsy and inadequate conducting technique. The author does not presume to establish in this work a technical system
which he considers the only means of achieving good musical results, but he does
attempt, by giving detailed and specific directions, to help establish the basic
rules of a correct technique.

There are many textbooks on conducting. Most of them offer valuable suggestions on the various aspects of the art, but there is a need for material
which thoroughly covers fundamental principles of technique. Skills must be mastered before the subtleties of musical expression can be validly established. Not
only do methods of managing technical problems need explanation, but the student
needs detailed exercises and selected musical examples for practice and for the
mastery of the expression of different musical values. A graded course of study
attempting to supply the ways and means of learning to conduct is attempted in
the present work. Technical skill will be developed step by step and adequate
technical exercise material will be supplied for the purpose. Just as important

will be the selected musical examples illustrating the various problems being
studied. It is hoped that by this twofold method of procedure the student may be
enabled more quickly to bridge the gap between mere rhythmic or metric time beating and its musical application. Beats in themselves are meaningless and must be
adapted to musical expression. This plan of progressive technical development
also will include corrective exercises to aid in the improvement of faulty technique. Development of skill in rhythmic dexterity will proceed from the most fundamental elements of baton technique to the complicated rhythms of modern music.
Special problems will be dealt with as units in themselves and then applied to selected musical examples. The study of the manipulation of the baton as it is applied to various measure beats and various combinations of these beats will be
studied extensively so that the student may be assured of having an adequate technical foundation for the expression of musical feeling through gesture. Musical
examples of contrasting styles will be suggested in order to enable the student to
vary his technique to suit the needs of different types of musical expression.

In connection with the studies outlined above and to be developed in the
present work, it is suggested that the student survey the field from other points
of view.

Most of the older contributions to the literature on the technique of conducting may be dismissed from consideration as practical student aids, even though
many of the important facts pertaining to conducting can be found therein. Richard
Wagner, for instance, (8,20) maintains that, "The whole duty of a conductor is
comprised in his ability always to indicate the right tempo," and that, (8,19)
"The right comprehension of the melos[1] is the sole guide to the right tempo." The
idea that the ability to set the correct tempo alone covers the technical qualifications of a conductor cannot be accepted today.

Hector Berlioz wrote at length on the status of conducting and orchestral
playing in his day, emphasizing (1,1) the importance of the efficient conductor as
the intermediate agent between composer and audience. He most critically enume-
rates the duties and qualifications of the conductor and truly states (1,20) that
"if he [the conductor] is inert and frozen,---- he paralyzes all about him, like
those floating masses of the polar seas, the approach of which is perceived
through the cooling of the atmosphere." In his description of the conductor's
time-beating activities, probably the first attempt to describe this technical
procedure, there is no attempt to outline a method of procedure whereby students
may learn. His beat diagrams only indicate the general direction of the beats by
arrows, and these are old fashioned and inadequate.

Of the modern contributions to the field, the very short handbooks by
Boult (2) and Kendrie (5) are of exceptional merit within their intended scope.
Each offers valuable suggestions which will be considered during the course of the
present work.

Albert Stoessel's Technique of the Baton (7) provides short melodic musical examples without harmonic background to be used in the practice of the various
beats. His suggestions on the solution of many problems of baton technique make
this book a valuable aid for students.

Two of the outstanding figures in the field of school music have contributed works on conducting. Will Earhart (3) was the first to build a book around
the principle that differing types of musical expression demand differing types of
gesture within given beat patterns. The present work attempts to develop this important principle still further through the use of musical examples of contrasting

_____

[1]Melody in all its aspects.

types selected to give the student practice in varying given beat patterns to suit
the needs of differing types of expression.

Gehrkens (4) gives many practical suggestions on the management of the
many problems which confront the conductor in the public school field.

Probably the outstanding modern textbook of conducting is the Handbook of
Conducting by Hermann Scherchen (6). It is a work which every serious student of
conducting should study thoroughly. The book, however, does presuppose a thorough
knowledge of the fundamentals of conducting. Concerning the elementary technique
of conducting, he says (6,154) "The methods of beating 1, 2, 3, or 4 in a bar must
be recognizable from the very first movements made. One cannot overstress the importance of the student's acquiring, by steadfast practice, an unambiguous method
of carrying out these metric divisions best suited to his idiosyncrasies." The
student should practice this elementary technique of conducting and it is hoped
that in the present work, material for the purpose can be found.

Many other more subtle factors making up the sum total of the conductor's
art, vaguely termed "good musicianship", "forceful personality", etc., are more
intangible and therefore more difficult to acquire. It is hoped that this study
can present much to the serious student which may prove of practical help in these
respects. It is necessary first, however, to separate mere technical and mechanical gesture from musical context, and study it as a unit in itself, and then attempt, for study purposes, to apply it immediately to musical expression. This,
then, will be the first objective,--the development of a perfect and automatic baton technique which must be so perfectly mastered that it may be relegated completely to the background of consciousness when administrative functions and the
needs of musical interpretation demand full attention.

Many teachers of music refuse to adhere to the accepted rules of conducting technique, directional patterns being ignored, and the rhythm of words and
syllables taking precedence in gesture over intelligible metric indications. The
author has observed many apparently skillful teachers resort to meaningless and
curious circular and angular gestures which greatly detract from the music being
performed, even though the performance may otherwise be enjoyable.[2] It is the author's contention that musical meaning can be clearly and adequately imparted
within the confines of the definitely established and universally understood con-
ventional sign language of conducting. The necessity for good conducting technique is instantly apparent when orchestral accompaniments are required for choral
performances. Much good playing and singing would be more readily enjoyed if the
conductor were rendered less conspicuous to his audience. It is hoped that many
may be aided in obtaining through the following studies the conductor's ideal--
"the ears of the audience and the eyes of the orchestra." (2,21)

Foreign symphony orchestra conductors of the virtuoso type should not concern us greatly. Many of them have grossly exploited music for self-glorification.
America has been invaded by many foreign musicians who have secured much acclaim
for themselves by resorting to cheap baton exhibitionism and cheap publicity made
up of legendary tales of what is politely called temperament. This condition is
still to be deplored. It is hoped that this book may be of some help in the process of teaching our own students to conduct our own orchestras and choruses, and
in assisting the American conductor finally to come into his own as the competent
interpreter of our own music.

---

[2]The circular gyrations of some conductors have caused these gentlemen to be called "pretzel
conductors". (5,7)

Chapter II

THE TECHNIQUE OF CONDUCTING

"The object of technique in all art is the achievement of the desired end with the greatest simplicity and economy of means."[1] (2,7) This dictum aptly applies to the art of conducting. The conventionalized sign language which has evolved through the years to meet the demands of complicated modern rhythmic devices, as well as the more sensitive renditions of the older music, is capable of being analyzed and explained. Such an analysis will make clear just how our "desired end" is reached with simplicity and economy of means. This technique, through the medium of which the conductor must recreate the composer's intention, must be learned, either by imitation or by practice and rational absorption, just as the instrumentalist must master the technique of his instrument.

A. GENERAL PRINCIPLES OF BATON MANIPULATION

Before actual practice is attempted, some general points applicable to all measure beats must be considered. Their importance cannot be overestimated.

1. The Preparatory or Cue-beat

An anticipatory up-motion must precede every attack of the orchestra or chorus, and if the ensuing musical sequence is rhythmic in nature it must be given in the tempo which is to follow.[2] A slow tempo should not be set by a quick preparatory beat and a quick tempo should not be set by a slow preparatory beat. This preparatory beat should be considered as the recoil, (described below), of the beat preceding the one on which the music begins, and should start on the same plane as that on which the ictus of the beat will be given. Exercises for the further study of an adequate preparatory motion preceding the starting beat will be presented later in connection with the attack. (p. 64) It will suffice now

---

[1] The conducting technique of past generations did not always achieve the desired end "with the greatest simplicity and economy of means." One interesting glimpse into the past seems worth quoting. Spohr in commenting on Beethoven's conducting method says, "It was Beethoven's custom to insert all sorts of dynamic markings in the parts, and remind his players of the marks by resorting to the most curious bodily contortions. At every sforzato he would thrust his arms away from his breast where he held them crossed. When he desired a piano he would crouch lower and lower; when the music grew louder into a forte, he would literally leap into the air and at times grow so excited as to yell in the midst of a climax." (7,3)

Berlioz also tells us that Habeneck, one of the acknowledged great conductors of the first half of the nineteenth century, conducted not from score but from a violin part. (9,7)

[2] Albert Coates used to admonish his pupils to take breath with the wind players when giving the preparatory up-beat.

4

in the earlier attempts at mechanical practice simply to precede the starting down-beat of every measure with an unprepared up-beat. This may be best thought of as the recoil of the last beat of an imaginary silent preceding measure of the same tempo.

2. The Beat Recoil

The ictus or point of every beat of every measure, although having direction and definite place in comparison with the other beats, has meaning only if the intermediary motions or beat recoils are adequately given. Failure to do this results in a putting of the stick in the various positions of beat placement, with the result that the beats lack point and rhythmic meaning. Earhart (3,13) has aptly presented this point as follows:

> The movement of a baton is largely a movement between beats or a movement that terminates in a beat; and it is followed by another movement that similarly terminates in another beat. What happens between beats (to the baton) is therefore of greater musical significance than the making of the beat itself; and it is the direction described by these movements between beats that impresses the eye as being the direction of the beats themselves.

3. Spatial Extent and Character of Beats

In the actual mechanics of time beating it must be remembered that all beats derive their size and character from the musical feeling of the sound being produced, and the exercises for study which follow are only outlines of directional patterns which must be modified and adapted to suit the needs of music if they are to become of intelligible musical worth. In general the size of beats is dependent on two factors, tempo and volume of sound. If a general rule can be made pertaining to the size of the beat, it might be stated that the slower the tempo, the larger the beat, and the louder the sound, the larger the beat. However, no such general rule could ever apply in all situations. With regard to the size of beats, the student should remember that the interval of time elapsing between each beat must be filled with motion, that the flow of the music must be continuous. If this principle is understood it will readily be seen that more time elapsing between beats will require a larger motion if the beats are not to be made so small that they are not rhythmically clear. The change of the size of the beat to govern the amount of sound is also dependent upon many other factors and no fast rule can be made to govern this principle. The type or character of the beats must be determined by the type or character of musical sound, and beats must be varied from short, vigorous, almost jerky motions, depicting that type of sound, to smoothly flowing gestures indicative of legato and cantabile types of expression. As our study proceeds mechanical exercises will be followed by suggestions for their musical adaptations in various types of style and tempo, and the student is cautioned again to realize that the beat diagrams to be given can only approximate what is appropriate in the actual conducting of music. It would be impossible to analyze for presentation in this work all of the diverse musical subtleties into appropriate gesture. In connection with the study of the many diversified musical examples suggested, the student's own musical sense must almost immediately make itself felt in the attempt to paint in motion a picture of the music he wishes to conduct.

Chapter III

THE PREPARATORY POSITION

A good preparatory position may definitely be considered as the first step in acquiring a good technique. The rendition of a musical composition may get off to a bad start and thereby be ruined irrevocably in consequence of poor preparation for the start on the part of the conductor. This may not only be due to a lack of an adequate preparatory beat or attack, but may be occasioned by the conductor's attitude, both physical and mental, even before a start is attempted. Therefore an adequate preparatory position is imperative. This position becomes the center of all movements in conducting.

The following procedure should be followed in establishing the preparatory position.

Exercise I

Place the right hand in front of the body, palm down, as if on the head of a child approximately chest high. The elbow should be slightly away from the body and there should be no exaggerated bending of the wrist or elbow.

Fig. 1
Correct preparatory
position of hand.

Fig. 2

Incorrect preparatory
hand position showing
exaggerated bend of
the wrist.

Fig. 3

Incorrect preparatory
hand position showing
exaggerated bend of
the elbow.

6

Exercise II

With the hand in the correct preparatory position, place the thumb along the ball of the stick,[1] parallel to it, letting the stick cross the first finger between its first and second joints, thereby bringing the ball of the stick into palm of the hand near the palm knuckle joint of the first finger. Curl the fingers about the ball or knob end of the stick so that the whole hand takes on a well-rounded and graceful appearance. In no case should the knuckle joints of the fingers be unduly prominent or should the little finger curl itself outward. Neither should the wrist bend in or out, thereby producing an angle with the forearm.

In the correct preparatory position the point of the stick should be directly in front of the body approximately on a level with the eyes. Boult, in this connection, (2,8) describes what he calls the "line of sight," which, "runs from the conductor's eye to the point of his stick and on to the eye of the particular player or the central or chief person of the group he is conducting." It is the author's experience that the point of the stick is usually somewhat higher than the "line of sight" unless an extremely high podium is adopted. The baton should be thought of as a prolongation of the arm, with no deviation to the right or left from the forearm. The grasp of the stick for exercise purposes should be light enough to assure flexibility of action, but firm enough to guard against a flabby and unauthoritative beat, the final determining factor being the weight and length of the beat demanded by the music to be performed. When wishing to start only a section of the orchestra or chorus, the whole body and eyes may be turned to that particular section. Some conductors assume a preparatory position in which the arms are extended full length on either side. This

Fig. 4   Fig. 5

The Correct Preparatory Position

[1]It is recommended that a balanced, knob or ball end baton be used. It should be light in weight and color and smoothly finished. For average use an eighteen-inch length is recommended, but for very large groups a slightly longer baton may prove more helpful.

Fig. 6
Incorrect preparatory
position showing unau-
thoritative curl of
the little finger

Fig. 7
Incorrect preparatory
position showing exag-
gerated upward bend of
the wrist

Fig. 8
Incorrect preparatory
position showing exag-
gerated angle between
baton and hand.

Incorrect Preparatory Positions

must be condemned, for in this position one side of the group cannot see the
stick at all. The student should guard against this common fault.
        The whole performance of a work may be ruined by a poor start, and a poor
start always results from poor preparation for the attack.

Chapter IV

THE TWO-BEAT MEASURE

The first beat of every measure is a down-beat, and the last beat of every measure (except for occasional final cut-off notes) is an up-beat. Therefore in the two-beat measure the general beat directions are down, up. However, as the following diagram of the path of the point of the stick attempts to indicate, the ictus or rhythmic point in time of the beat is followed by a recoil which serves to prepare for the second beat. The two-beat immediately falls back into the channel made previously by the first beat.

The Two-beat

Diagram 1.

In all beat diagrams, increasing speed of motion as the stick approaches the ictus, is indicated by a darker shading of the line. In certain kinds of gently flowing music the stick will often travel from beat to beat at the same rate of speed, but a definite rhythmic pulse for exercise purposes is difficult to attain without a definite culminating flick of the stick on each beat. The student is reminded again that beat diagrams can only approximate what is appropriate in the actual conducting of music, and that the mechanical exercises will be followed by suggestions for their musical adaptation in various types of style and tempo.

A. MECHANICAL EXERCISES ON THE TWO-BEAT FOR THE DEVELOPMENT OF RHYTHMIC CLARITY AND STYLE

Exercise 1

With a metronomic speed of approximately ninety beats per minute, make the point of the stick describe the motion indicated in the diagram, not forgetting to start with the preparatory beat previously described. Kendrie (5,6) describes the actual motion as follows: "Visible rhythm is best exemplified in the swing of the pendulum. Yet this swing itself is not regular, for it gains speed on the downward motion and loses it on the upward motion. Nevertheless, the exact instant when it touches the lowest part of its curve can be ascertained, for its regularity is constant."

Be sure that there is correct cooperation of the wrist, fingers, and the arm. This correct cooperation will involve:

a. A quick down-up motion of the wrist at the ictus or point of each beat which may be compared to the flick of the wrist used by children in playing yo-yo. This motion must never be thought of as a dropping of the hand from the wrist below the level of the forearm.

b. A down and out motion of the elbow and upper arm on the down-beat, and and in and up motion on the upbeat. This, of course, will not be a motion apart

9

from the lower arm and hand but will seem to carry the hand and stick with it on the recoil.

c. A movement of the stick in the hand in the channel between the thumb and first finger, the fingers which are curled about the ball of the stick thereby controlling the recoil.

- - - - -

An adequate mastery of the manipulation of this basic two-beat measure must be attained, for it will serve as a basis of beat style which will be applied to all beats. Of course, actual musical intent will determine the character and size of the beat, but all of these adaptations can be made later when the beat is applied to musical examples.

Chapter V

REASONS FOR FAULTY BEAT MANIPULATION WITH CORRECTIVE
EXERCISES

Difficulties in mastering the manipulation of the baton described in the last chapter are usually encountered because of certain specific and definite faults which beginning students are prone to make. An enumeration of these more usual faults and a careful checking on each point will greatly aid the student in ultimate mastery.

<u>1</u>. A dropping of the hand from the wrist at the point of the beat.

This most glaring feature of bad baton technique results in directing the eyes of the orchestra or chorus to the wrist, which becomes the highest point of interest at the instant the beat is given instead of the point of the stick.[1]

<u>a</u>. Corrective exercise for dropping the wrist.

<u>Without the stick</u> conduct the measure with an exaggerated high bend of the wrist, gradually attempting to put in the "flick" without dropping the wrist.

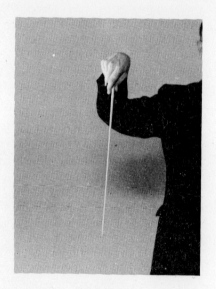

Fig. 9
Incorrect dropping of
the wrist on the down-beat

Fig. 10
Corrective exercise for
the dropping of the wrist

---

[1]It is interesting in contrast to note that Berlioz' directions for the two-beat measure are as follows: (1,4) "Two in a bar is beaten simply. The arm and the stick of the conductor are raised, so that his hand is on a level with his head, he marks the first beat, by dropping the point of his stick perpendicularly (<u>bending his wrist</u> as much as possible; and not lowering the whole arm), and the second beat by raising the stick by a contrary gesture."

2. Entire lack of the "wrist-flick," which produces a pump-handle type of beat with the whole arm.

   a. Corrective exercise for the lack of "wrist-flick" at the ictus of the beat.
   Try to recreate the motion of throwing a small rubber ball to the floor. Then without the stick describe the beat motion very slowly trying to include this "wrist-flick" at the point of the beat.

3. A lack of movement of the stick in the hand.
   This type of beat manipulation always results in a stiff and lumbering beat devoid of any flexibility and incapable of producing any kind of lilting expression.

   a. Corrective exercise.
   To overcome this tendency towards stiffness, let the point of the stick flick back and hit the shoulder after each second beat, without deliberately raising the hand for the purpose. This will result in a slight release of the knob in the hand by the fingers, thus forcing movement of the stick. The flabbiness of the beat produced by this action should not concern the student or teacher as the action can be tightened again when the extreme stiffness of the beat has been eliminated.

4. A too flabby motion of the stick in the fingers.
   This results in a beat lacking decisiveness and authority.

   a. Corrective exercise for too flabby beat.
   Eliminate the excess motion of the stick by tightening the grasp of the ball in the fingers.

5. A turning of the hand and forearm to the right on the recoil (See Fig. 11).
   This tendency is often more pronounced on the second beat of a three-beat measure or on the third beat of a four-beat measure.

   b. Corrective exercise for the incorrect turning of the hand.
   Without the stick describe the motion of the beat slowly, making sure that the palm is always down, and that the elbow takes on a decidedly out motion on the beat where the turning is most apparent.

6. The lack of cooperation of the elbow and the upper arm in the manipulation of the beat.
   This type of beat makes impossible the expression of music of any lilt or sweep.

   a. Corrective exercise.
   Without the stick practice a down-out, and in-up motion of the elbow and again attempt to correlate this motion with the hand and stick.

7. The tendency to place the two-beat in a place different from the one-beat, or the making of two separate beat channels.
   This presupposes an accent and should be eliminated.[2]

---

[2]See footnote on page 13.

Fig. 11

The Incorrect Turning of the Hand

    Kendrie (5,7) establishes what he calls the plane of the beat, and de-
scribes it as follows:

        Taking the lowest point in the curve as the instant when the
        "count" begins we are able to establish an imaginary plane
        on which all the succeeding "counts" (divisions of the meas-
        ure) are to be indicated. The "contact" of the motion,
        therefore, with this plane indicates the instant of the
        "count" (or beginning of the tone), while the movement <u>above</u>

_____

    [2]The two-beat advocated by Albert Coates always was placed higher than the one-beat, in this
manner,--

Diagram 2

resulting, in my opinion, in unevenness and lack of symmetry.

the plane, away from it and toward it, indicates both duration and intensity.

This is a very useful procedure for study purposes but in actual practice
the plane varies so constantly to meet the needs of musical expression, both in
accentuation and in dynamic gradation of tone, that an arbitrary insistence on
the maintenance of this plane would, it seems, lead to a less flexible technique.
Furthermore, as will presently be explained, the compound measures, especially
nine and twelve, actually place the last three beats on a higher plane. But, for
the student who is continually varying the plane of each beat with no apparent
reason for doing so, this exercise of maintaining the same plane will prove of
great corrective value.

a. Corrective exercise.
Place an object such as a music stand on a level with the "plane" of the
beat and let the point of the stick touch this artificially established plane on
every beat.

8. The tendency for the stick to slip up in the hand.

a. Corrective exercise.
Start conducting with the stick held in the middle and gradually work the
stick down in the hand until the ball is once more in the palm of the hand.

9. The tendency of excessive bodily movement in connection with the beat.
If violence of gesture or overconducting is continually resorted to, the
orchestra is apt to become insensitive to more subtle and refined motions. The
greatest economy of means should always be employed to produce the desired result.
In connection with a word of caution on the matter of bodily movement should also
be mentioned the common tendency of bending the knees with every beat or of beating time with the foot. The student should carefully refrain from all of these
unnecessary bodily movements.

It is now recommended that the student apply this two-beat technique
(which now should be thoroughly corrected as a pattern) to various tempi, both
slow and fast, conducting in imagination (perhaps with the metronome) various
types of music, both legato and staccato. Scherchen (6,151) speaks of these two
basic types of conducting as follows:

> There are two fundamental types of gestures used in conducting;
> namely, a quick movement completed in the shortest possible
> time, and a movement long drawn out. These correspond to the
> two elementary opposites, legato and staccato (i.e., notes ex-
> tended to a maximum and notes reduced to a minimum). Extended
> notes must be articulated into periods, cantabile; short notes
> must be organized rhythmically. The slow gestures presenting
> the melody, correspond to extended notes, and the quick ges-
> tures outlining rhythmic groups, to short notes.

An explanation of what actually happens to differentiate one type of direction from another is difficult. The student should try to feel the expressive
qualities of the differing types of music suggested in the next chapter, and vary
the beat according to the musical feeling.

Chapter VI

METHODS OF PROCEDURE FOR THE STUDY OF MUSICAL EXAMPLES
AND MUSICAL EXAMPLES FOR THE TWO-BEAT MEASURE

A. <u>Methods of procedure</u>.

There are several methods of procedure which may prove helpful to the student in his first attempt to express music by means of the baton. Phonograph records of selected musical examples should prove valuable aids, not only as model reference guides in interpretation and score reading, but as a means of accompanying conducting practice. This somewhat Dalcrozian method of attempting to depict in gesture the rhythmic and musical values one hears, is, of course, not true conducting at all, and should only serve as a means of help in capturing musical values. Some students need the stimulus of the sound of actual music to aid self-conscious physical efforts. The connection between the auditory image of a printed page and gestures for its expression in sound is sometimes not easy to establish. Any means taken to facilitate the process of establishing this connection justify the end. The suggestion is offered, therefore, that the student conduct while listening to recordings of the following musical examples, trying to feel, and to portray in the beat, the style of the music being played. When the student has learned to express the desired musical feeling by the beat, he should conduct the same piece of music to a pianist, trying constantly to imagine an orchestra or chorus under direction. True musical direction of the orchestra should not be attempted until the student has captured the musical spirit of a work and is able to express it by gesture. Knowledge of the score must precede any attempt to conduct.

B. <u>Musical examples to be used for study purposes in the two-beat measure</u>.

<u>TYPE I</u>
<u>Slow or Moderate, Heavy, and Rhythmic</u>

Example 1
War March of the Priests from "Athalia" - Mendelssohn
Victor recording, No. 7104,
Piano reduction, Carl Fisher, Inc., N.Y.

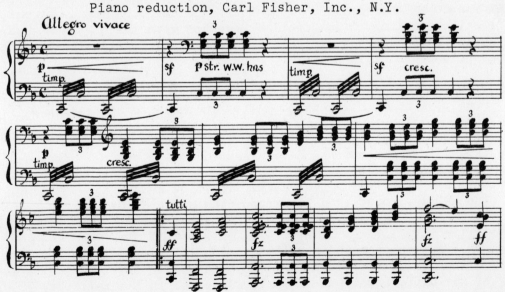

Example 2
Rakoczy March - Berlioz
Victor recording, No. 6823
Piano reduction, Carl Fischer, Inc., N.Y.

The student should not be concerned at this point in his studies with the problem of the incomplete first measure. These problems in attack will be presented later. (p. 67)

Example 3
Overture to "The Flying Dutchman" - Wagner
Victor recording, No. 6547
Piano reduction, Carl Fischer, Inc., N.Y.

Example 4
Introduction to the Third Act of "Lohengrin" - Wagner
Victor recording, No. 7386
Piano reduction, Carl Fischer, Inc., N.Y.

In the type of musical expression exemplified by the examples above a very vigorous flick of the beat at the ictus is demanded, with more time elapsing between these vigorous beats. This duration of time is filled in with a continuous slower motion, which is not broken except for purposes of secondary accentuation. The actual beat in the above examples is produced with more speed than the beat of the following example.

TYPE II
Slow, Legato, Flowing

Example 5
Morning from "Peer Gynt Suite No. 1" – Grieg
Victor recording, No. 11834
Piano reduction, G. Schirmer, N.Y.

In this type of expression, the pendulamic[1] swing of the stick is much more regular, gaining less speed in the downward motion and losing less on the upward motion. There is also a much less pronounced beat flick. This may lead to a somewhat wider arc of the swing.

TYPE III
Moderately fast, Staccato, Rhythmic, Military Precision

Example 6
March – "The Stars and Stripes Forever" – Sousa
Victor recording, Nos. 1441, 20132, 35805
(Other Sousa marches contained on the backs
of these records may also be used.)
Piano reduction, Theodore Presser Co., Phil.

---

[1]Word coined by Kendrie (5,7)

The beat for this type of music should be much smaller and on a slightly higher plane. Because less time elapses between beats at this tempo, a large beat would destroy the crispness and quick precision demanded by this type of music and would make it ponderous and heavy. The beats should be small, vigorous, and without much recoil.

TYPE IV
Moderately fast, Lilting, and Graceful

Example 7
Shepherd's Dance from "Three Dances from Henry VIII" - German
Victor recording, No. 22171
Piano reduction, Carl Fischer, Inc., N.Y.

Example 8
Country Dance from "Nell Gwynn" - German
Victor recording, No. 9009
Piano reduction, Carl Fischer, Inc., N.Y.

A continuation of this example will bring a much slower tempo and a more lilting character in the music.

In the above example a light, lilting beat is demanded, much in the manner of Type II examples, but faster and with much more "lift," which is produced by more recoil from the beats than in the Type II examples.

TYPE V
Very fast, with Rhythmic Precision, but not too Vigorous

Example 9
Overture - Die Entführung aus dem Serail - Mozart
Victor recording, No. 7822
Piano reduction, Carl Fischer, Inc., N.Y.

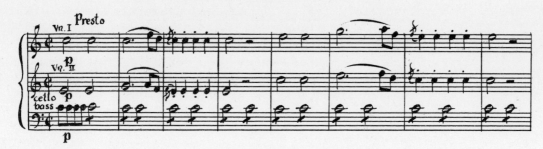

Example 10
Overture - Figaros Hochzeit - Mozart
Victor recording, No. 11242
Piano reduction, Carl Fischer, Inc., N.Y.

In this very rapid music, the recoil of the one-beat is apt to be very much less pronounced, the two-beat therefore having little or no preparation. As Earhart (3,10) describes this beat there is hardly a definite stroke on the second beat and "the up-beat becomes a mere return to the position from which the down-beat started."

Chapter VII

THE THREE-BEAT MEASURE

An adequate knowledge of the basic principles of beat manipulation as explained in connection with the two-beat measure can be applied to all the other conventionalized beat directions, and as the student progresses much less time

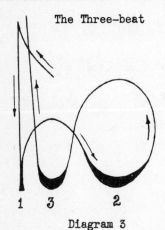

The Three-beat

Diagram 3

should be needed for mechanized beat practice. As progress is made in knowledge of beat form, the working of the stick should become automatic and should not require continuous conscious direction.

The general form of the three-beat measure is down, right, up,[1] but again, as in all beats, the motion between the beats is the important matter. (Refer again to p. 5)

In all beats right or left of center the faulty tendency of turning the hand is apt to be more pronounced. The student should analyze his beat with special care on this point (see note and illustration on p. 13), as well as all the other faults of manipulation enumerated in connection with the two-beat.

- - - - -

A. MECHANICAL EXERCISES ON THE THREE-BEAT FOR THE DEVELOPMENT
OF RHYTHMIC CLARITY AND STYLE

Exercise 1

The same procedure as before should be followed, i.e., first conducting to the metronome at various tempi and in various styles. Then the following sequence exercises should be studied in tempo.

Exercise 2
Rhythmic examples for clarity in beat differentiation

a. Keep the value of the quarter note constant.

1. 2 2 3 3	3. 2 2 2 2	5. 2 2 3 3	7. 2 3 2 2
4 4 4 4	2 2 4 4	2 4 2 4	4 2 4 2
2. 2 3 2 3	4. 3 3 3 3	6. 3 2 2 3	8. 3 2 3 2
4 4 4 4	2 2 4 4	2 4 2 4	4 2 2 4

---

[1]Berlioz remarks (1,5), "When the conductor faces the players, it is immaterial whether he marks the second beat to the right, or to the left."

This is interesting historically. The old-fashioned left direction for two, still occasionally used by some Italian band conductors, is not to be considered.

b. Keep the value of the eighth note constant.

1. 2 2 2 3 3 3   3. 3 2 3 2 3 2   5. 3 2 2 3 3 2   7. 3 3 2 2 3 3
   8 4 2 8 4 2   4 8 2 4 8 2   8 4 8 2 4 2   4 8 2 8 4 2

2. 2 3 2 3 2 3   4. 2 3 3 2 2 3   6. 2 3 3 2 3 2   8. 2 2 3 3 2 2
   8 8 4 4 2 2   8 2 4 8 2 8   2 8 4 8 2 4   8 4 2 8 8 4

B. MUSICAL EXAMPLES FOR THE THREE-BEAT-MEASURE

TYPE I
Moderately fast, Legato

Example 11
Symphony in B-minor (First movement) - Schubert
Victor recording, No. 6663-6665
Piano reduction, Carl Fischer, Inc., N.Y.

TYPE II
Moderately fast, Vigorous, Rather heavy, Decisive

Example 12
Excerpt from Symphony in B-minor (First Movement) - Schubert

TYPE III
Quick and Flowing

Example 13
Overture to "Egmont" (Allegro) - Beethoven
Victor recording, No. 7291
Piano reduction, Carl Fischer, Inc., N.Y.

Some conductors take this _allegro_ in one. This "uncontrollable allegro-rush" is condemned by Weingartner (9,14), and its further implications are discussed.

Example 14
Symphony No. 3 (First movement) - Beethoven
Victor recording, No. 7439-7445
Piano reduction, Carl Fischer, Inc., N.Y.

TYPE IV
Fast, Rhythmic, Light, Graceful

Example 15
Poupee Valsante - Poldini
Victor recording, No. 20668
Piano, G. Schirmer, N.Y.

Example 16
Anitra's Dance from "Peer Gynt Suite No. 1" - Grieg
Victor recording, No. 11835
Piano reduction, Carl Fischer, Inc., N.Y.

The two preceding examples go best at a tempo lying just between a one and a three, and might conceivably go better at times in one than in three. Earhart (3,16) discusses the possible treatment of variations of the fast three-beat as follows: "At still faster tempo, and with still less emphasis attached to the second and third beats, the second beat becomes shorter and more upward in direction."

TYPE V
Moderately slow, Vigorous

Example 17
Mignon Overture - Ambroise Thomas
Victor recording, No. 6650
Piano reduction, Carl Fischer, Inc., N.Y.

TYPE VI
Vigorous, Waltz time

Example 18
Excerpt from The Bat - Johann Strauss
Victor recording, No. 8651
Piano reduction, Carl Fischer, Inc., N.Y.

Reproduced from "The Bat" by Strauss
by permission of the copyright owners,
G. Schirmer, Inc., New York

No better material can be selected for the study of tempo changes in the three-beat measure than the Strauss Waltzes. A clear line of demarcation between the one- and the three-beat is impossible. The true waltz tempo if unvaried has a better lilt in one, but the constant changes in nuance and accentuation make necessary a clear and decisive baton technique in the change. The student is referred for further study to p. 78 of Albert Stoessel's Technique of the Baton. (7)

TYPE VII
Slow, Contemplative, Religious

Example 19
Overture to "Tannhäuser" - Wagner
Victor recording, No. 7262
Piano reduction, Carl Fischer, Inc., N.Y.

Example 20
Symphony No. 3 - Mendelssohn
Columbia recording, No. 67671-D

TYPE VIII
Very Slow, Flowing

Example 21
Largo from "Xerxes" - Handel
Victor recording, No. 6648
Piano reduction, Carl Fischer, Inc., N.Y.

Chapter VIII

THE FOUR BEAT MEASURE

No further directions for style in mechanized time-beating exercises will be given. The student is referred constantly to the directions and fault correction exercises on pp. 11-14. These directions should be applied to the study of all beats.

The Four-beat

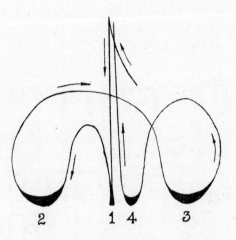

2   1 4   3

Diagram 4

A. EXERCISES FOR THE DEVELOPMENT OF RHYTHMIC CLARITY
AND BEAT DIFFERENTIATION

a. Keep the quarter note constant.

<pre>
1. 2 2 3 3 4 4 4 4 3 3 2 2
   4 4 4 4 4 4 4 4 4 4 4 4

2. 2 3 4 4 3 2
   4 4 4 4 4 4

3. 2 4 3 4 4 2 3 2
   4 4 4 4 4 4 4 4
</pre>

b. In the following exercises keep the eighth note constant.

<pre>
1. 2 2 2 2 2 3 3 3 3 3 4 4 4 4 4
   8 4 2 8 4 2 8 4 2 8 4 2 8 4 2
</pre>

26

2. 2 3 4 4 3 2 3 2 4 2 4 3
    2 8 4 2 8 4 2 8 8 4 4 2

3. 2 4 3 4 4 2 3 2 3 2 4 2 2 3 4 2
    4 2 8 4 8 8 2 4 8 2 8 2 4 8 8 2

B. MUSICAL EXAMPLES FOR THE FOUR-BEAT MEASURE

TYPE I
Slow, Vigorous, Sustained

Example 22
Overture to "Die Meistersinger" - Wagner
Victor recording, No. 6651
Piano reduction, Schott

TYPE II
Fast, Vigorous

Example 23
Finale from Symphony in E Minor (The New World) - Dvorak
Victor recording, No. 8740
Piano reduction, Carl Fischer, Inc., N.Y.

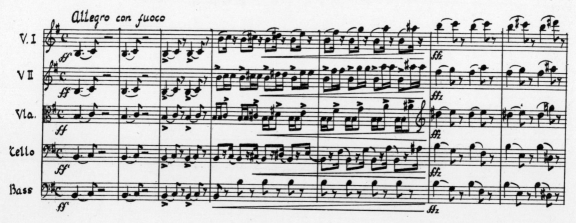

Example 24
Finale from Symphony No. 4 - Tschaikowsky
Victor recording, No. 6933
Piano reduction, Carl Fischer, Inc., N.Y.

TYPE III
Moderately fast, Flowing

Example 25
Finale from Symphony No. 1 - Brahms
Victor recording, No. 8971-8975
Piano reduction, Carl Fischer, Inc., N.Y.

TYPE IV
Fast, Light, Flowing, Forte

Example 26
Overture to "Euryanthe" - von Weber
Victor recording, No. 9398
Piano reduction, Carl Fischer, Inc., N.Y.

The above example is properly conducted in two.

TYPE V
Slow, Ponderous, Heavy, Rhythmic precision

Example 27
Procession of the Holy Grail from "Parsifal" - Wagner
Victor recording, No. 8617, 8618
Piano reduction, Hawks, London

TYPE VI
Slow, Legato, Flowing

Example 28
Excerpt from Overture to "Der Freischütz" - von Weber
Victor recording, No. 6705
Piano reduction, Carl Fischer, Inc., N.Y.

The type of beat required for the above example is difficult to master for it requires a very slow rhythmic indication in which the duration of sound between beats must be covered by motion, but in which the beats themselves must be well defined.

TYPE VII
Fast, Light, Staccato

Example 29
Symphony No. 6, Third movement – Tschaikowsky
Victor recording, No. 7294-7298
Piano reduction, Ditson, Boston

TYPE VIII
Very Slow, Flowing, Pianissimo

Example 30
Excerpt from the Overture to "Euryanthe" – von Weber
Victor recording, No. 9398
Piano reduction, Carl Fischer, Inc., N.Y.

Chapter IX

THE FIVE-BEAT MEASURE

As stated previously, there should be only one down-beat and one up-beat in any measure. Therefore, the older method of beating five as <u>two and three</u> or <u>three and two</u> is not recommended. Conduct the five-beat measure as follows, depending on the grouping of the notes within the bar:

<u>A</u>. <u>THE FIVE-BEAT WITH SECONDARY ACCENT FALLING ON THE THIRD BEAT</u>

<u>B</u>. <u>THE FIVE-BEAT WITH SECONDARY ACCENT FALLING ON THE FOURTH BEAT</u>

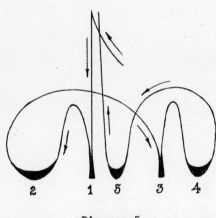

Diagram 5

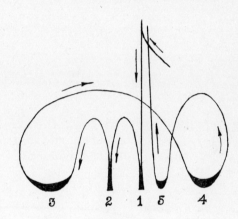

Diagram 6

When the tempo is so fast that it is not expedient to beat out every beat in the bar, the measure should be conducted in an uneven two, with the first beat covering either two or three counts depending on the grouping. Some very fast measures in five are conducted one in a bar, particularly when there does not seem to be a secondary accent in the measure. Such measures are usually not continuous in a composition and usually occur only in modern music. Numerous examples can be found in Stravinsky's "Petrouchka" or "Le Sacre du Printemps." If the nature of the orchestration is so intricate as to demand the giving of every beat in the measure and the tempo is uncomfortably fast for this, the beat should be managed almost entirely by the hand and fingers, the stick moving freely in the hand, and the motion of the arm being almost entirely eliminated.

<u>C</u>. <u>EXERCISES FOR THE DEVELOPMENT OF RHYTHMIC CLARITY AND BEAT DIFFERENTIATION</u>

1. Conduct $\frac{5}{4}$ as a grouping of two and three at different tempi.

2. Conduct $\frac{5}{4}$ as a grouping of three and two at different tempi.

31

3. Alternate these two $\frac{5}{4}$ beats at every measure.

4. 2 3 4 5 5 (change) 4 3 2
   4 4 4 4 4   4 4 4

5. 2 4 3 5 5 (change) 3 4 2
   4 4 4 4 4   4 4 4

6. With the metronome set at 180 conduct $\frac{5}{8}$ in two as a grouping of two and three. Each click represents an eighth note.

7. With the metronome set at 180 conduct $\frac{5}{8}$ in two as a grouping of three and two, each click representing an eighth note.

8. Alternate these two beats on every bar.

9. With the eighth note constant at 180 conduct the following:

$$
\begin{array}{cccccccc}
2 & 5 & 2 & 5 & 2 & 5 & 2 & 5 \\
4 & 8 & 4 & 8 & 4 & 8 & 4 & 8
\end{array}
$$

D. MUSICAL EXAMPLES TO BE STUDIED WITH THE FIVE-BEAT MEASURE

No further attempt will be made to present music for the purpose of studying different "types" of expression.

Example 31

1. The five-beat measure as a grouping of two and three

Allegro from Symphony No. 6 - Tschaikowsky
Victor recording, No. 7294-7298
Piano reduction, Carl Fischer, Inc., N.Y.

Diagram 7

Some conductors conduct this movement effectively in the manner shown in Diagram 7, the first and second beats, owing to the musical phrase, being merged in one long beat. Earhart says (3,82) concerning the type of beat to be used in conducting this music, "The beat is characteristically a 'dry' beat, and while dynamics must be indicated there is little need for striking any beat with a heavy impulse."

2. The five-beat measure as a grouping of three and two

Example 32
Mars, the Bringer of War from "The Planets" - Holst
Columbia recording, No. 67384-D

Reproduced from "Mars" in the Suite "The Planets" by Holst
by permission of the copyright owners, The Curwen Company, London.

This music, largely percussive and barbarous in character, demands a vigorous, heavy beat, as contrasted with the beat style of the preceding example.

Example 33
"Egyptienne" from Silhouettes - Henry Hadley
Carl Fischer, Inc., N.Y.

Reproduced from "Egyptienne" in the Suite "Silhouettes"
by Hadley. Copyright 1919 by Carl Fischer, Inc.,
New York. International copyright secured.

Example 34
Excerpt from <u>Petrouchka</u> - Stravinsky

Reproduced from "Petrouchka" by Stravinsky
by permission of the copyright owners,
Galaxy Music Corporation, New York.

　　　The five-eight measures in the preceding example are usually conducted
one in a bar.

Chapter X

THE SIX-BEAT MEASURE

The following diagrams indicate different methods of conducting the six-beat measure:

The Six-beat

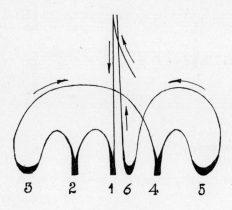

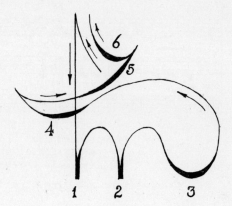

Diagram 8   Diagram 9

Some conductors prefer the type of six-beat indicated in Diagram 9 as being more symmetrical. This method may be extremely useful for conducting music at a faster tempo, which may at times call for a merging of the beats into a two-beat measure. It is particularly useful in making a ritard from a two-beat to a six-beat when it seems necessary to divide the last half of the measure. For ordinary usage, however, the writer favors the first way (diagram 8) for it places the beats equally distributed right and left of center.

The six-beat measure in two has already been considered.

A. RHYTHMIC EXERCISES

1. Conduct $\frac{6}{8}$ or $\frac{6}{4}$ according to the first diagram at varying tempi. Be sure that the sixth beat falls into the channel of the first beat.

2. 2 3 4 5 6 6 5 4 3 2
   4 4 4 4 4 4 4 4 4 4

3. 2 4 6 6 4 2
   4 4 4 4 4 4

4. 2 4 3 5 4 6 6 4 5 3 4 2
   4 4 4 4 4 4 4 4 4 4 4 4

35

5. With the metronome set at 120 conduct alternately two and six, in the two-beat letting three clicks of the metronome equal one beat and in the six-beat conducting every click.

6. With the metronome set at 140 conduct the following exercise, the metronome clicks representing eighth notes:

$$
\begin{array}{cccccccccccccc}
2 & 6 & 3 & 5 & 4 & 3 & 2 & 3 & 5 & 2 & 4 & 6 & 6 & 4 & 2 \\
4 & 8 & 2 & 8 & 4 & 2 & 4 & 2 & 4 & 2 & 8 & 8 & 4 & 2 & 4
\end{array}
$$

B. MUSICAL EXAMPLES

Example 35
Calm as the Night – Bohm
Victor recording, No. 1752
Piano reduction, Carl Fischer, Inc., N.Y.

Example 36
Andante from Symphony in G minor – Mozart
Victor recording, No. 8883-8885
Piano reduction, Carl Fisher, Inc., N.Y.

Example 37
Prelude to Liebestod - Wagner
Victor recording, No. 1169
Piano reduction, Hawks, London

Example 38
Excerpt from "Mignon" - Thomas
Victor recording, No. 6650
Piano reduction, Carl Fischer, Inc., N.Y.

Chapter XI

THE SEVEN-BEAT MEASURE

A grouping of <u>four and three</u> or of <u>three and four</u> is most common in this infrequently used rhythm. If the music is at a tempo requiring the giving of every beat, the measure is conducted as follows:

<u>A</u>. <u>THE SEVEN-BEAT WITH THE SECONDARY ACCENT FALLING ON FOUR</u>

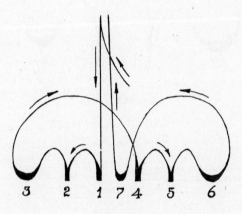

3   2   1 7 4   5   6

Diagram 10

<u>B</u>. <u>THE SEVEN-BEAT WITH THE SECONDARY ACCENT FALLING ON FIVE</u>

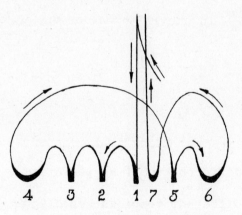

4   3   2   1 7 5   6

Diagram 11

Quite conceivably a grouping of <u>two, two, and three</u> may be employed, in which case the beats may be given thus:

<u>C</u>. <u>THE SEVEN-BEAT WITH SECONDARY ACCENTS FALLING ON THREE AND FIVE</u>

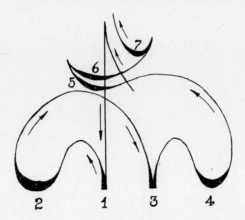

Diagram 12

<u>D</u>. <u>THE SEVEN BEAT AS UNEVEN TWO OR THREE</u>

In modern music we frequently find various groupings of eighth notes in the 7/8 bar at a fast tempo. These should be conducted according to their grouping as follows:

1. $\frac{4}{8}$ plus $\frac{3}{8}$ in uneven two.

2. $\frac{3}{8}$ plus $\frac{4}{8}$ in uneven two.

3. $\frac{2}{8}$ plus $\frac{2}{8}$ plus $\frac{3}{8}$ in uneven three, or any other combination of grouping in an uneven three.

<u>E</u>. <u>RHYTHMIC EXERCISES</u>

1. Conduct $\frac{7}{4}$ at different tempi as per diagram 10.

2. Conduct $\frac{7}{4}$ at different tempi as per diagram 11.

3. Conduct $\frac{7}{4}$ at different tempi as per diagram 12.

4. With the eighth note represented by metronomic clicks at 180 conduct the following, beating three to the measure as indicated by the grouping of notes:

Example 39

5. 5 7 3 2 7 4 7 5 3 2 4
   4 4 4 4 4 4 4 4 4 4 4

6. With the eighth note unit remaining constant, conduct the following:

3 4 6 2 5 7 4 3 5 6 2 4 7 7 5 3 4
4 8 8 2 8 4 4 2 8 8 4 4 8 4 2 4 4

F. MUSICAL EXAMPLES

Example 40
Excerpt from Symphony No. 2 – Randall Thompson

Example 41
Excerpt from Symphony No. 1 - Randall Thompson

Example 42
Motet - Psalm CVIII, O God, My Heart is Ready - George Henry Day
Pub. Clayton F. Summy Co.

Chapter XII

THE EIGHT-BEAT MEASURE

The eight-beat measure usually occurs as a compound or subdivided four and should be conducted in the following manner:

<u>A</u>. THE EIGHT OR COMPOUND FOUR-BEAT

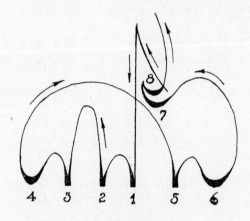

Diagram 13

It is quite conceivable that modern music might demand the continuous pounding of reiterated notes, eight to the bar, without secondary accents. If the tempo is slow enough in this case to demand giving a beat on each count, it should be done in the following manner:

<u>B</u>. THE EIGHT-BEAT MEASURE WITHOUT SUBDIVIDING THE BEATS

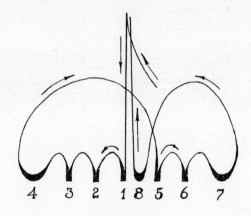

Diagram 14

The above pattern would lend itself to variation for any unusual grouping of notes within the bar, such as three plus three plus two, etc. Such exigencies, however, are so rare that further consideration of them seems unnecessary.

C. RHYTHMIC EXERCISES

1. Conduct $\frac{8}{8}$ as divided four at varying tempi.

2. Conduct four at 60 and eight at 120 alternating each bar. Be sure that in the slow four the motion is continuous and flowing but that there is a definite flick on each beat.

3. Conduct from memory the following sequence:

$$\frac{2\ 4\ 3\ 5\ 4\ 6\ 5\ 7\ 6\ 8\ 8\ 6\ 7\ 5\ 6\ 4\ 5\ 3\ 4\ 2}{4\ 4\ 4\ 4\ 4\ 4\ 4\ 4\ 4\ 4\ 4\ 4\ 4\ 4\ 4\ 4\ 4\ 4\ 4\ 4}$$

4. With a constant eighth note as the unit, conduct the following:

$$\frac{2\ 5\ 3\ 6\ 4\ 7\ 6\ 4\ 3\ 5\ 8\ 6\ 8\ 8\ 5\ 3\ 4}{4\ 8\ 4\ 8\ 4\ 8\ 8\ 4\ 2\ 8\ 4\ 8\ 8\ 4\ 8\ 2\ 4}$$

D. MUSICAL EXAMPLES

Example 43
Air – J. S. Bach
Victor recording, No. 7484
Piano reduction, Carl Fischer, Inc., N.Y.

Example 44
Symphony No. 2 - Schubert

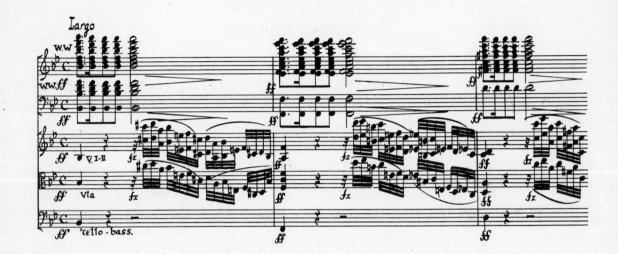

Chapter XIII

THE NINE-BEAT MEASURE

The nine-beat measure is usually a compound measure and should be thought of as a divided three. It is usually conducted as follows (see first diagram):

The Nine-beat

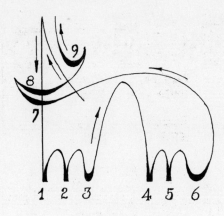

Diagram 15

The Incorrect Nine-beat

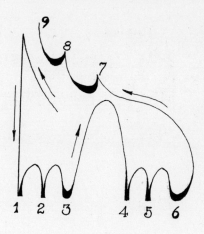

Diagram 16

Many conductors place the secondary beats of one (the two and three) on the left of the center. Such a procedure, in my opinion, does not follow basic ternary rhythm as well. If, however, an accent or very sharply marked fourth beat is indicated, such a procedure would be more apt.

Avoid the tendency to conduct the seven, eight, and nine in the same direction (see second diagram above). This manner of conducting the nine-beat is confusing because there are three up-beats in the measure.

A. RHYTHMIC EXERCISES

1. Conduct $\frac{9}{8}$ or $\frac{9}{4}$ at varying tempi.

2. In a $\frac{9}{8}$ measure conduct in three at $\quad$ = 50, and in nine at $\quad$ = 150, alternating each bar. Be sure that in the slow three the motion is continuous and flowing but that there is a definite flick on each beat.

3. Conduct from memory the following sequence:

$$\frac{2}{4}\ \frac{3}{4}\ \frac{5}{4}\ \frac{4}{4}\ \frac{6}{4}\ \frac{5}{4}\ \frac{7}{4}\ \frac{6}{4}\ \frac{8}{4}\ \frac{7}{4}\ \frac{9}{4}\ \frac{9}{4}\ \frac{7}{4}\ \frac{8}{4}\ \frac{6}{4}\ \frac{7}{4}\ \frac{5}{4}\ \frac{6}{4}\ \frac{4}{4}\ \frac{5}{4}\ \frac{3}{4}\ \frac{4}{4}\ \frac{2}{4}$$

4. With a constant eighth note as the unit conduct the following:

45

6 7 4 5 3 6 9 2 7 9 9 6 3 5 2 6 4
8 4 8 8 4 8 8 4 8 4 8 8 4 8 2 8 4

B. MUSICAL EXAMPLES

Example 45
Sorcerer's Apprentice – Dukas
Victor recording, No. 7021
Pub. Durand, Paris

Example 46
Afternoon of a Faun – Debussy
Victor recording, No. 6696
Pub. Fromont, Paris

A consideration of the two preceding examples will show that in Example 45, the secondary beats falling on four and on seven should be indicated with greater preparation in order to assure good ensemble, while in Example 46 the whole measure should be conducted with a very even flowing sequence of beats. Example 45 is often conducted in three.

Chapter XIV

OTHER DIVIDED MEASURES

Any measure may be divided if in so doing the interests of clarity and better ensemble are served.   It is unusual, however, to find music demanding continued use of the divided measure, the division usually being employed in a ritard of sufficient magnitude to demand additional rhythmic direction.   The beat of any measure should not be divided unless the orchestra needs this extra impulse to aid in attaining better ensemble. The student should be warned not to fall into the habit of continually beating notes instead of beats. Some con- ductors aiming to secure greater clearness and security by continually dividing the beat actually do just the opposite and greatly annoy the players by overcon- ducting.[1]

The following illustrations will serve as examples of divided measures:

A. THE DIVIDED TWO-BEAT   B. THE DIVIDED THREE-BEAT

   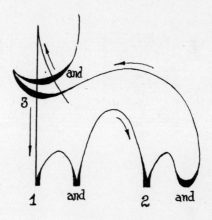

Diagram 17   Diagram 18

---

[1]Often beats should be merged rather than divided, e.g., an eight-beat measure in an accele- rando may attain such a rapid tempo that it will go better in four.

C. THE DIVIDED SIX-BEAT

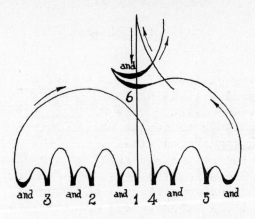

Diagram 19

D. RHYTHMIC EXERCISES

1. Conduct as follows, in sequence:
Divided two, divided three, divided four, divided five, divided six, repeat divided six, and back to divided two.

2. With metronome at $\quad\!$ = 60 conduct:
$\frac{2}{2}$, $\frac{2}{2}$ divided, $\frac{3}{2}$, $\frac{3}{2}$ divided, etc., up to six and backwards.

3. With metronome at 100 for the quarter note, and dividing all of the half-note unit measures, conduct the following:

3 4 2 4 4 5 3 4 6 2 4 3 4
2 4 2 8 2 4 2 4 4 2 8 2 4

E. MUSICAL EXAMPLES

Example 47
Excerpt from "Irish" from Silhouettes - Hadley
Pub. Carl Fischer, Inc., N.Y.

Divided three

Reproduced from "Irish" in the Suite "Silhouettes" by Hadley, Copyright 1919 by Carl Fischer, Inc., New York. International copyright secured.

Example 48
Symphony No. 6 – Haydn

Divided three

Chapter XV

THE TEN- AND ELEVEN-BEAT MEASURES

The ten- and eleven-beat measures occur so seldom that we may pass over them very quickly. The knowledge of conducting these measures is useful however for exercise purposes. When these measures actually occur in music they are usually in fast tempo with uneven groupings within the bar, and should be conducted according to the grouping of the notes.

The following illustrations will serve as examples of various note groupings which could be conducted in an <u>uneven four-beat measure</u>.

<u>A</u>. <u>TEN-EIGHT IN FOUR</u>

Do not conduct triplets. The eighth note remains constant.

Example 49

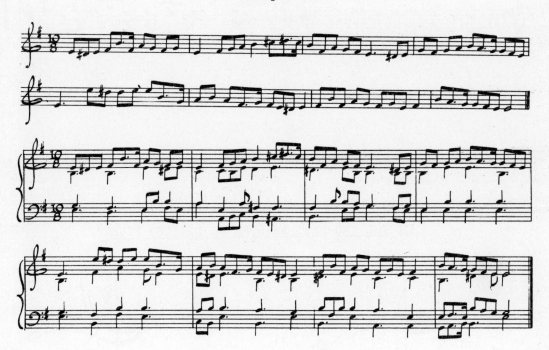

<u>B</u>. <u>ELEVEN-EIGHT IN FOUR</u>

Do not conduct triplets. The eighth note remains constant.

Example 50

For exercise purposes in the actual ten and eleven beats, the following beat outlines will suffice.

C. THE TEN-BEAT MEASURE AS DIVIDED FIVE

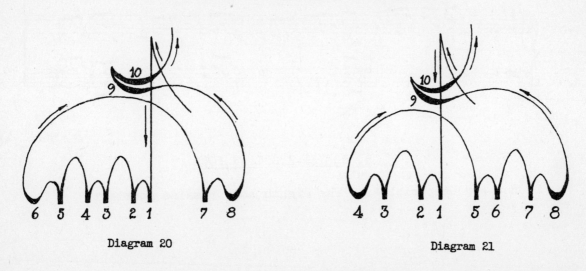

Diagram 20   Diagram 21

<u>**D.**</u> <u>**THE ELEVEN—BEAT MEASURE AS THREE PLUS THREE PLUS THREE PLUS TWO**</u>

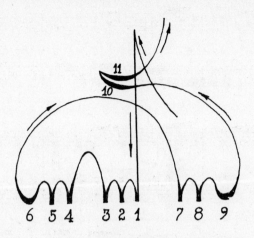

Diagram 22

Chapter XVI

THE TWELVE-BEAT MEASURE

The twelve-beat measure may be thought of as a compound four.

The Twelve-beat Measure

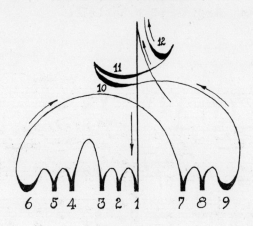

Diagram 23

A. RHYTHMIC EXERCISES

1. Conduct $\frac{12}{8}$ at 120 to the eighth note.
2. Conduct four at ♩. = 30 and twelve at ♪ = 120, alternately.
3. Conduct 3 6 9 12 12 9 6 3 <u>from memory</u>.
          4 4 4 4 4 4 4 4
4. With the value of the eighth note constant, conduct $\frac{6}{8}$ in 6, $\frac{6}{8}$ in 2,
$\frac{9}{8}$ in 9, $\frac{9}{8}$ in 3, $\frac{12}{8}$ in 12, $\frac{12}{8}$ in 4.

B. RHYTHMIC SEQUENCE EXERCISES TO BE CONDUCTED FROM MEMORY

1. 2 4 3 5 4 6 5 7 6 8 7 9 8 10 9 11 10 12 and backwards to 2.
2. 2 5 3 6 4 7 5 8 6 9 7 10 8 11 9 12 and backwards to 2.

The ability to conduct the two exercises above at a fairly rapid tempo <u>from memory</u> with no mistakes in beat direction will demonstrate the mastery of automatic beat manipulation insofar as it pertains to direction. While these exercises are mechanical, the mental process involved in doing them is similar to that of reading a score and conducting. Physical action, at least, must take place automatically, without conscious direction, the mind being occupied solely with what is happening and what is about to happen in the music, both rhythmically

and from the standpoint of interpretation. The student is urged to practice
these exercises diligently until complete mastery is achieved.

C. MUSICAL EXAMPLE

Example 51
Concerto for two violins - J. S. Bach
Victor recording, No. 7732, 7733
Pub. Breitkopf & Härtel

Chapter XVII

THE ONE-BEAT MEASURE

The one-beat measure seems, for many, to be the most difficult to conduct with facility. In order to develop this feeling for the unit with one motion, I suggest that the one-beat should be felt first as a circle. Practice de-
scribing a complete circle with the stick, increasing the speed of the motion as
the bottom of the circle is reached. It should be practiced both clockwise and
counterclockwise, the motion gradually being brought into a more elliptical shape,
as follows:

Preparatory Exercises for the One-beat

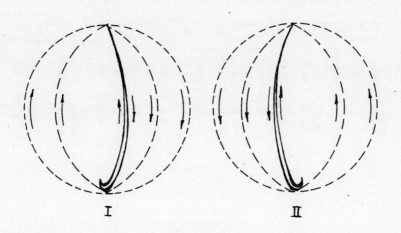

I   II

Diagram 24

This motion should finally result in a definite down-up motion, the beat
being produced by a "flick" at the plane of the beat and the hand and arm being
drawn up to the original position in a more relaxed manner.

A rather difficult tempo to execute in a one lies just on the verge of a
fast three. This may be conducted by combining two and three to the right and upward, after the heavy down-beat has been given. (See p. 24) Probably this type
of beat would not be used continuously but serves admirably in bridging the gap in
the change from a one into a three in a ritard. The slower the tempo of the measure the more pronounced will become the indication of two and finally of three.
A sequence of beats indicating a ritard from a one-beat measure into a three-beat
measure might be outlined as follows:

Ritard from a One into a Three

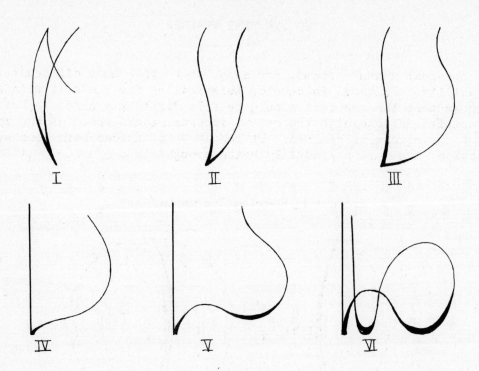

Diagram 25

Some conductors advise giving a series of one-beats in slightly different directions to avoid monotony. The Beethoven scherzi, for example, fall easily into definite measure groupings and the first beat of each bar may become a concealed four or three. Every beat, of course, must remain a down-beat.

A. RHYTHMIC EXERCISES FOR THE ONE-BEAT

1. Conduct $\frac{3}{8}$ in one at $\eighthnote$ = 180.

2. Conduct $\frac{3}{4}$ in one at $\quarternote$ = 120.

3. With metronome set at 90 to the dotted half-note, beat alternately $\frac{3}{4}$ in three, and $\frac{3}{4}$ in one.

4. With the eighth note constant conduct the following:

$\frac{6}{8}$ in six, $\frac{6}{8}$ in two, $\frac{9}{8}$ in nine, $\frac{9}{8}$ in three,

$\frac{3}{8}$ in three, $\frac{3}{8}$ in one, $\frac{12}{8}$ in twelve,

$\frac{12}{8}$ in four

5. With metronome giving the constant eighth note conduct the following:

$$\frac{2}{4} \; \frac{5}{8} \; \frac{3}{8} \; \frac{6}{8} \; \frac{7}{8} \; \frac{4}{4} \; \frac{8}{2} \; \frac{5}{4} \; \frac{6}{8} \; \frac{9}{8} \; \frac{3}{4} \; \frac{6}{2} \; \frac{2}{8} \; \frac{7}{8} \; \frac{5}{8} \; \frac{9}{8} \; \frac{12}{8} \; \frac{2}{2} \; \frac{8}{4} \; \frac{4}{4}$$

B. MUSICAL EXAMPLES

Example 52
Scherzo from Midsummer Night's Dream – Mendelssohn
Victor recording, No. 7080, 9283, 6676
Piano reduction, Carl Fischer, Inc., N.Y.

Example 53
Furiant from "The Bartered Bride" – Smetana
Pub. G. Schirmer, N.Y.

Example 54
Scherzo from Symphony No. 6 – Beethoven
Victor recording, No. 6939-6943
Edition Peters for two pianos

Chapter XVIII

THE LEFT HAND

The gaining of freedom and fluency in the use of the left hand is worthy of diligent study, for the manner in which a conductor uses his left hand is highly indicative not only of his experience but also of his very success as an interpreter. The left hand must perform many duties in conducting, which we shall attempt to analyze and separate for study. It must be remembered that from the technical and mechanical point of view absolute ambidexterity must be acquired in order that the conductor be free to express himself in music by gesture. This is the primary purpose of much of the stereotyped exercise material to follow. It is the author's belief that technical perfection in the exercises here given will greatly help the student to free himself to express musical values to the limit of his musical ability.

A. THE USE OF THE LEFT HAND AS A TIME-BEATING AGENT

The left hand as a time-beating agent should be sparsely used, its qualitative and expressional functions being of more importance. But, the need for added emphasis and added power of control often makes it desirable to use the left hand as a reënforcing agent. It is therefore recommended that the first studies in the use of the left hand should be rhythmic. When used in conjunction with the right hand for time-beating purposes, the left hand is used in exactly opposite directions left and right.

B. LEFT-HAND EXERCISES

1. With the left palm always down, conduct all the measures with both hands together and then
2. With the left hand alone.
A few of the beats are diagrammed to serve as examples for all of the left-hand beats.

Left-hand Beat Directions

The Three-beat

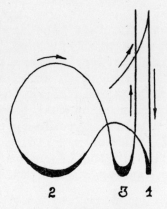

Diagram 26

The Four-beat

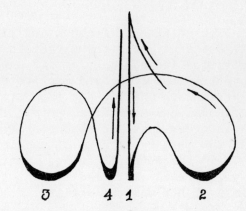

Diagram 27

The Six-beat

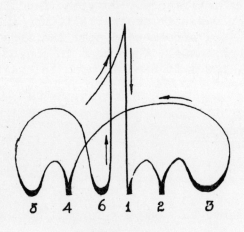

Diagram 28

The Nine-beat

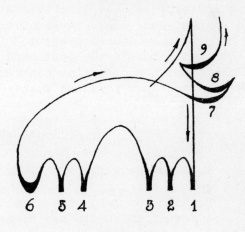

Diagram 29

3. Proceed through all the beats from two to twelve consecutively, alternating between left and right hand with each bar. The hand not in use should remain in the preparatory rest position.

<u>C</u>. <u>THE USE OF THE LEFT HAND FOR INDICATING CRESCENDO AND DIMINUENDO</u>

Any purely arbitrary rules for the dynamic or expressional uses of the left hand are difficult to give, for the very subtlety and spontaneity which should be characteristic of these functions is often destroyed by the conscious effort of portraying them. However, if the following rather stilted exercises can help the student to learn to use his hands independently of one another they will be valuable.

The crescendo may be indicated in two ways--by increasing the size of the beat and by raising the level of the plane of the beat. Sometimes these indications for the increased amount of sound happen separately but more usually together. To approximate this musical usage of the left hand, conduct the following exercise:

1.   Example 55

With the palm turned up, begin to raise the left arm and hand at the moment the beats begin. Maintain the highest level of sound for four beats, the three and four of the second measure and the one and two of the third measure. Then turn the hand over and bring it down again to indicate the diminuendo.

The process of progression in the exercise might be illustrated as follows:

Fig. 12   Fig. 13

1. Beginning of crescendo   2. Climax of crescendo

Fig. 14   Fig. 15

3. Beginning of diminuendo   4. Close of diminuendo

2. Practice the same type of exercise varying the beat as follows:

Example 56

The difficulty in mastering these exercises seems to lie in achieving absolute independence of action of the two hands. The student is cautioned to re-refrain from accompanying the beat motion of the right hand with any rudimentary beat movements of the left hand. This involuntary and subconscious nervous reflex simply shows a lack of separate left-hand technique.

It is also important that the raising of the hand in the crescendo should not be done too spasmodically or quickly, so that the climax is reached too soon. Regarding this Weingartner says, (9,6)

> Even our best orchestras of today need to be constantly told that the increase and decrease of tone is to be done evenly and gradually, not suddenly; and the difficulty of doing this increases with the number of bars over which these variations in volume have to be extended. "Diminuendo signifies forte, crescendo signifies piano," said Bülow. "This is only a seeming contradiction, since to play forte at the beginning of a crescendo, and piano at the beginning of a diminuendo, really means the negation of crescendo and diminuendo."

The movement should be gradual and truly indicative of the effect wanted. The beat itself may become larger or more agitated during the crescendo and smaller again gradually as the diminuendo is in progress. This may be accompanied by a raising and lowering of the plane of the beat.

D. THE USE OF THE LEFT HAND FOR INDICATING THE SUBITO PIANO AND THE SUBITO FORTE OR SFORZANDO

The uses of the left hand in indicating these dynamics are mainly preparatory, and the signals should be given always in anticipation of the desired effect. If a sudden subsidence of sound is desired, an abrupt bringing of the left hand across the body with the palm turned outwards, towards the orchestra, immediately after the last fortissimo beat is given, should secure the desired effect. By all means avoid the "crouching pianissimo."

For the indication of a sudden explosive increase in sound the clenched fist may be raised from the plane of the beat immediately after the last beat preceding the change has been given and then brought down vigorously with the right hand.[2]

3. Exercises for the development of technique in indicating the subito forte and piano.

Example 57

---

[2] This technique will be more completely described in connection with the accent.

Example 58

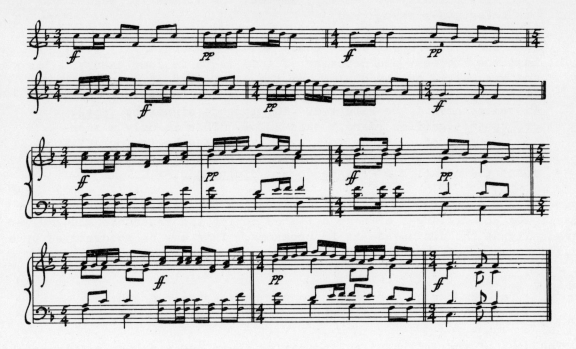

Example 59

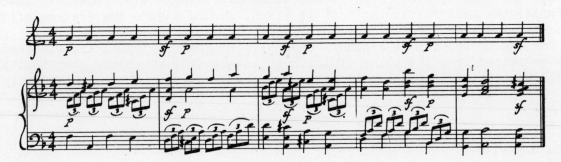

Example 60

E. MUSICAL EXAMPLES

Examples 61, 62, and 63 are taken from The Overture to <u>Rosamunde</u> (Zauber-harfe) - Schubert

Example 61

Example 62

Example 63

Example 64
Excerpt from Overture to <u>Egmont</u> - Beethoven

F. THE USE OF THE LEFT HAND FOR INDICATING ENTRANCES

Kendrie (5,29) sums up the matter of the giving of cues for entrances as follows:

> Entrances for separate sections occasionally are also given
> with the left hand by first establishing the "line of sight"
> from the forefinger to the particular group and then giving
> the entrance with a complete preparatory motion (in the rhythm
> of the motions which the right hand is making).

A word of warning might be added regarding the overanxious cueing in of important or difficult solo entrances. The player is always anxious to do his best in concert and if his entrance is made clear by a glance he will appreciate being left alone to take care of his own particular musical duty. In discussing this point Kendrie further states (5,29) that

> entrances for the most part are given with the eye alone, and
> occasionally a slight forward movement of the baton toward the
> section or player in question. Too frequent left-hand indica-
> tions simply demoralize an orchestra to the point where nobody
> comes in unless scooped in, while, per contra, with a better
> routined organization an unexpected left-hand signal can scare
> a good player out.

G. OTHER LEFT-HAND USES

In radio and theater work, there are times when signals must be given during a performance to take care of exigencies which arise at the moment. When the exact timing of a radio program has been destroyed because of interpolated items or some other cause, it is often necessary to cut out repeats or to leave out del segno indications. Second endings may be indicated by holding up two fingers until the ending is reached. A stop at an appropriate place in the music other than the ending may be indicated by raising the clenched fist as a warning and by bringing it down firmly on the concluding beat.

Chapter XIX

THE ATTACK

Some famous conductor has stated that the most difficult thing to do is to start an orchestra and that the next hardest thing to do is to stop it. It is almost daily demonstrated in the conducting class that the statement carries a grain of truth, for the most serious shortcomings of the inexperienced conductor are usually those arising from a lack of adequate preparation for the attack and the release. The reason for this fault is basically probably a psychological one arising from the fact that the student does not, in imagination, place himself in the place of the singer or player he is conducting. If the conductor will adopt a mental attitude of actually imagining himself as producing the tones desired from the players or singers, the basis for the technique of preparation becomes firmly established. Take breath with the singers or wind players on the preparatory motion and give time for bow manipulation to string players.

A. THE ATTACK ON THE BEAT

The following exercises are for practice in the attack when the music begins on a definite beat of the measure. Start the preliminary motion as an upbeat (without preparation), thought of as a recoil from the last beat of an imaginary preceding measure.

Exercise 1
For starting on the first beat
of a measure

Exercise 2
For starting a three-beat measure
on the second beat

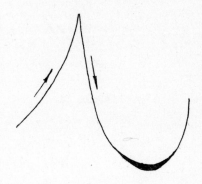

Diagram 30   Diagram 31

66

Exercise 3
For starting a four-beat measure
on the second beat

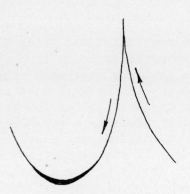

Diagram 32

Exercise 4
For starting a four-beat measure
on the third beat

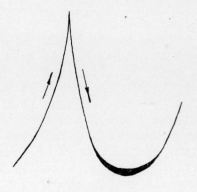

Diagram 33

Exercise 5
For starting any measure on its
last beat

Diagram 34

Exercise 6
For starting a six-beat measure
on the fifth beat

Diagram 35

Exercise 7
For starting a nine-beat measure on
its seventh beat

Diagram 36

Other examples of a similar nature should be devised and practiced by the student so that facility in starting on any beat of any measure is acquired.[1] This should be practiced at all tempi and with different types of sound in mind, legato, staccato, piano, forte, etc.

B. THE ATTACK AFTER THE BEAT

The attack for starts which do not occur exactly on the beat requires different treatment. Usually the giving of an unprepared complete beat is sufficient, the sound being produced after the beat is given. Scherchen (6,161) suggests that

> in order to insure accuracy of performance here, let the conductor's left hand, raised to the height of the right hand ready for the down-beat, perform an accurate up-beat gesture. Then the right hand may start beating the "one" of the bar as written, taking on from the left hand, so to speak, the preparatory up-beat which has tended towards it.

The following examples will illustrate this type of attack:

Example 65
Excerpt from <u>Ruy Blas</u> - Mendelssohn

Example 66
<u>Don Juan</u> - Strauss

Reproduced from "Don Juan" Opus 20 by Strauss
by permission of the copyright owners,
C. F. Peters, Leipzig.

---

[1] For practice in large classes the author has occasionally formed the class into two groups facing each other and has directed each group to conduct alternate measures in a two to twelve sequence, the group not conducting at the moment waiting in rest position and picking up the beat as a preparation on the last measure being conducted by the other group, and continuing.

C. THE ATTACK AFTER THE UP-BEAT

Music which starts preceding the down-beat may be given an adequate attack indication by giving an unprepared complete up-beat.

The following will serve as examples for this type of technique.

Example 67
Excerpt from Rosamunde (Zauberharfe) - Schubert

Example 68
Excerpt from Oberon - Weber

For another example of this type of start refer to Example 2, on page 16.

D. THE ATTACK FOR SUSTAINED HOLDS

The attack for sustained holds sometimes requires the immediate raising of the baton after the beat is given, especially if a diminuendo is indicated as in the following example:

Example 69
Overture to Egmont - Beethoven

The attack should always be given on the beat plane and never by thrusting the arms into the air as some conductors are wont to do in this instance.

If the attack is pianissimo followed by a crescendo, the gradual raising of the baton and left hand can be employed.

Chapter XX

THE FERMATA AND RELEASE

An adequate preparation for the release is just as important as it is for the attack. The sudden bringing down of the stick at the conclusion of a fermata, without preparation, is never conducive to a good release. The sound of t-t-t-t-t-t- or s-s-s-s-s-s- making its way about the chorus because of poorly executed endings can be avoided if proper release preparation is given.

If the fermata continues forte or crescendo to the end and is not followed by other entrances, a vigorous down-stroke for the cut-off is called for, but this must be preceded by an upward preparatory motion similar to the preparatory motion of the attack. The following diagrams will illustrate methods of making the release.

<u>A</u>. <u>EXAMPLES OF RELEASE</u>

1.   2.   3.

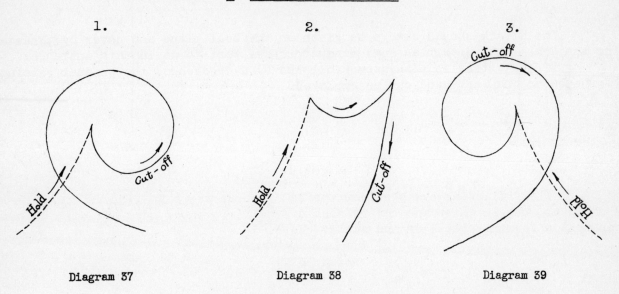

Diagram 37   Diagram 38   Diagram 39

4.

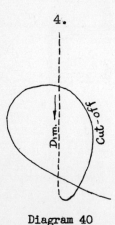

Diagram 40

If the effect of a fading out or dying away of the sound is called for, the hands may be brought slowly downward and together, and if any release is needed, a very deliberate motion of this kind may be used: (See diagram 40.)

The avoidance of too abrupt a release is always best in soft endings resulting from a diminuendo.

When a fermata occurs which demands a vigorous cut-off and yet is followed by other entrances needing preparation, it is better to arrange the cut-off so that the baton is in position and ready for the attack to come. This will preclude any misunderstanding resulting from the necessity of raising the baton again to the preparatory position. Diagram 37 will illustrate this.

71

The following examples should serve admirably for the study of this technique.

Example 70
Overture to The Magic Flute - Mozart

Method of attack and release for the above example.

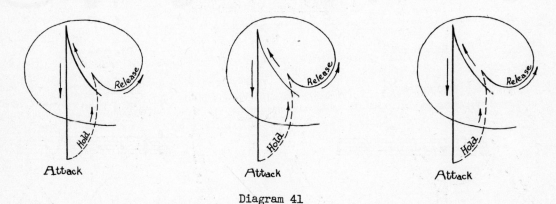

Diagram 41

In the following example from the same source the same type of technique is employed, but in this case the release of the first chord must act also as the preparation for the attack of the second chord.

Example 71

B. COMBINING THE RELEASE WITH THE PREPARATION FOR THE NEXT BEAT

In combining the release with the preparation for the next beat when no rest or distinct breaking of the sound occurs, it is necessary to make a sustaining motion on the fermata and a preparatory motion for the cut-off, the cut-off then acting as the preparation for the following beat. For study purposes a four-four measure should be dissected and practiced with sustained holds on every beat, as follows:

Example 72
The hold on one

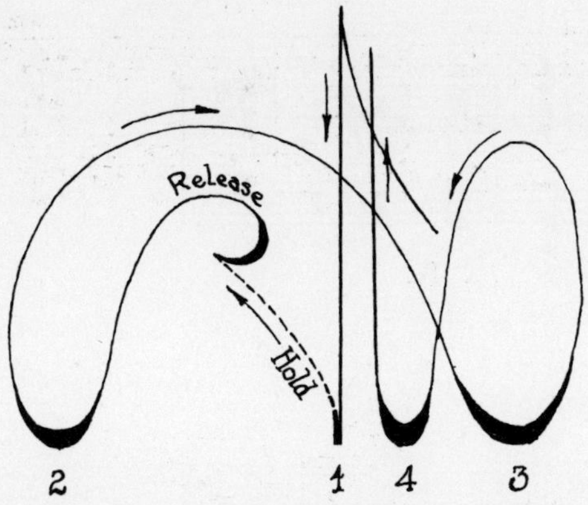

Example 73
The hold on two

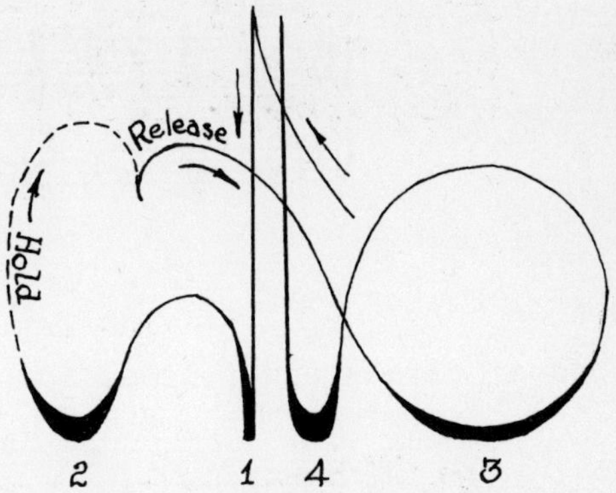

Diagram 42

Diagram 43

Example 74
The hold on three

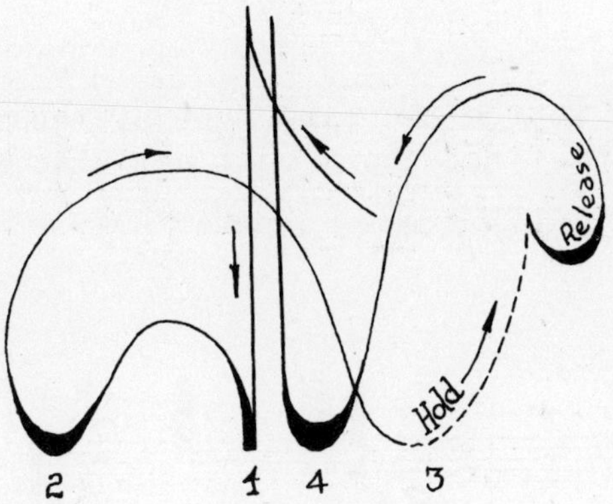

Example 75
The hold on four

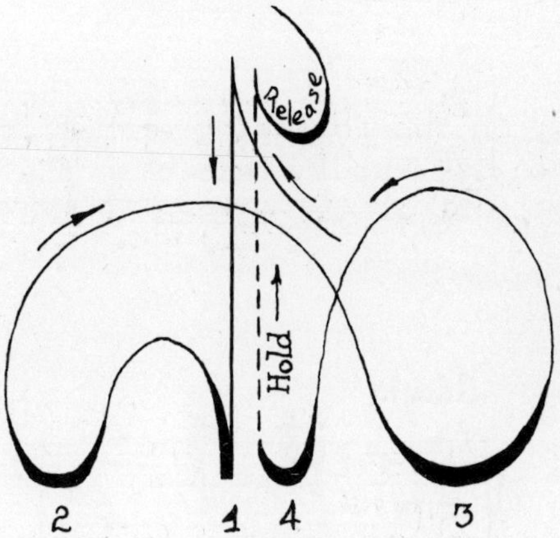

Diagram 44

Diagram 45

Musical examples illustrating the above technique may be found in nearly all of the Bach Chorals, a few of which are here selected for study purposes.

Example 76
Traurigkeit - J. S. Bach

Example 77
O Gott, du frommer Gott – J. S. Bach

Example 78
Alles ist an Gottes Segen – J. S. Bach

Example 79
Was frag' ich nach der Welt – J. S. Bach

Example 80
Nun Prieset Alle – J. S. Bach

Insofar as is possible the stick should be kept moving to indicate sustained sound during a fermata. If the stick is held motionless a diminution in
amount of tone is apt to occur.

Chapter XXI

THE RITARD AND ACCELERANDO

It is often necessary to divide or to merge beats in a ritard or an accelerando. The following exercises are devised to aid the student in changing beats smoothly to meet these demands. A diligent study of them is recommended until all tendency to make an abrupt and disconcerting change disappears.

A. EXERCISES FOR THE DEVELOPMENT OF A SMOOTH TECHNIQUE IN THE RITARD AND ACCELERANDO

1. Start conducting a $\frac{3}{4}$ measure in one at 180 to the quarter note and gradually and smoothly slacken the speed until a three is indicated in feeling. At the point where the change begins to occur great care should be taken that the ritard remains even and unbroken. The one should work gradually into a partial three and finally into a complete three with recoils for each beat. Refer again to the diagrams on p. 55.

2. Start conducting a $\frac{3}{4}$ measure in three at 100 to the quarter note and in like manner make a smooth accelerando until the beat is changed into a one. This exercise reverses the procedure of exercise 1.

3. Start conducting a $\frac{6}{8}$ measure in two at 132 to the dotted quarter. Ritard smoothly from a two into a six, as indicated by the following diagrams.

The Ritard from a Two into a Six

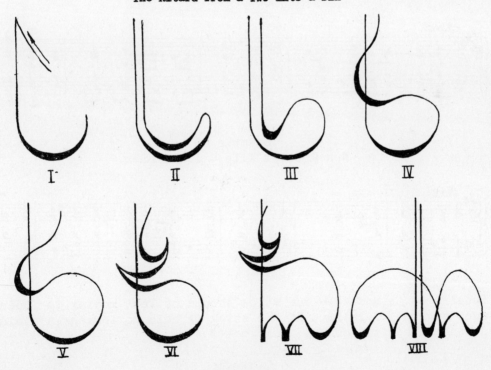

Diagram 46

75

4. In like manner develop an accelerando from a six into a two, reversing exercise 3.

5. Start conducting in nine and make a smooth accelerando into a three. Vary this exercise so that the division may take place on any beat of the measure.

6. Reverse exercise 5, making a smooth ritard from a three into a nine.

7. In the same manner make a smooth accelerando from a twelve into a four.

8. In the same manner make a smooth ritard from a four into a twelve.

Chapter XXII

THE ACCENT

While the mechanical technique of giving the accent has been dealt with to some extent in our consideration of the subito forte, a more detailed analysis of this technique should be undertaken. It has again to do entirely with the matter of preparation. In general, the accent on any particular beat must be indicated <u>before</u> that beat by giving a larger recoil from the preceding beat. Thus, an accent on the first beat of the measure would require a larger preparatory beat, thought of as a larger recoil from the last beat of the preceding measure. In like manner an accent on the second beat of the measure would require a larger recoil from the first beat, etc.

<u>A.</u> <u>EXERCISES FOR THE STUDY OF THE TECHNIQUE OF THE ACCENT</u>

1. Example 81
The accent on one

2. Example 82
The accent on two

Diagram 47

Diagram 48

3. Example 83
The accent on **three**

4. Example 84
The accent on four

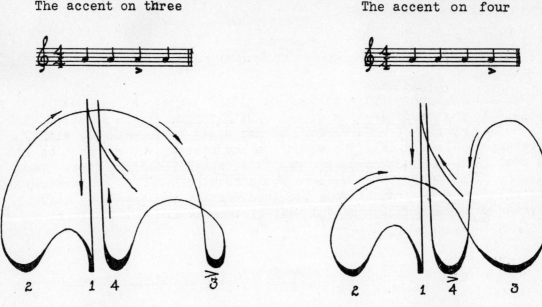

Diagram 49
Diagram 50

5. Continue this type of study until practice is obtained in accenting every beat of every measure.

6. a. Conduct a two to twelve sequence placing an accent on the first beat of every measure.

b. Conduct a two to twelve sequence placing the accent on the second beat of every measure, etc.

7. Conduct a two to twelve sequence placing the accent on the last beat of every measure.

8. Conduct a two to twelve sequence placing the accent on the next to the last beat of every measure.

The cooperation and coordination of both hands in the technique of the accent is necessary. Refer again to pages 61 and 62 studying the musical examples with this purpose in mind.

B. OFF-BEAT ACCENTS

When accents occur in parts of the measure other than those receiving the beat, a different treatment must be employed. In some cases, primarily when the music is slow enough to warrant, a vigorous division of the accented beat may be given. Usually, however, a vigorous accented beat on the beat preceding the accent will achieve the result. Examples of this are given below.

Example 85
Excerpt from <u>The Magic Flute</u> - Mozart

The above example is, of course, conducted in two, the accents falling on the last half of the second beat.

Example 86
Excerpt from the scherzo of Symphony No. 3 – Beethoven

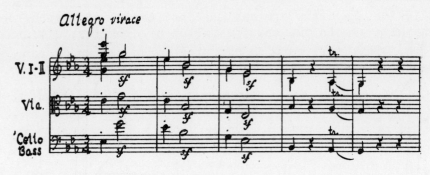

Example 87
Excerpt from Symphony No. 2 – Beethoven

Another example will be found on p. 56, <u>The Furiant</u> from "The Bartered Bride" by Smetana.

Chapter XXIII

ADDITIONAL TECHNICAL EXERCISE MATERIAL

The following exercises are designed to furnish additional material for the study of rhythmic precision, the indication of dynamics, divided beats, accents, holds, etc. They will furnish material for a review of some of the purely technical elements of conducting.

Exercise 1

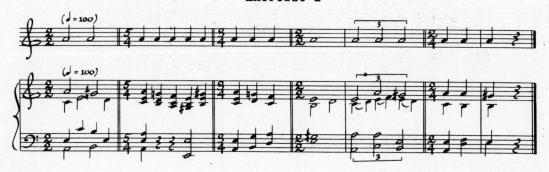

Exercise 2

Exercise 3

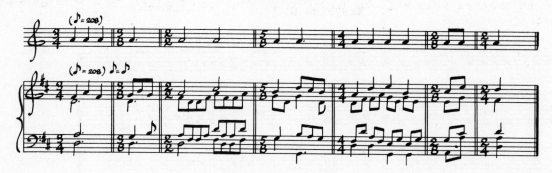

Exercise 4

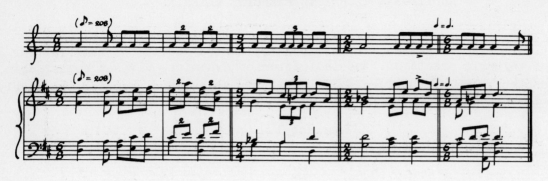

Exercise 5

Exercise 6

Exercise 7

Exercise 8

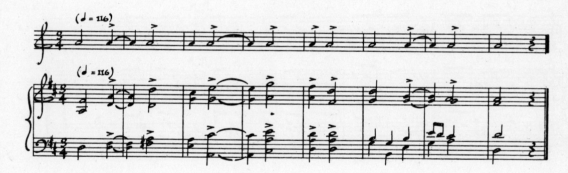

Exercise 9

Exercise 10

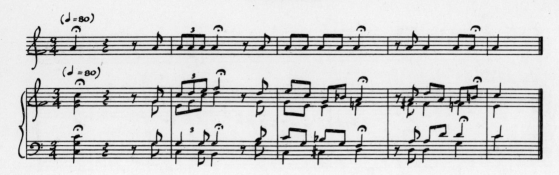

Exercise 11

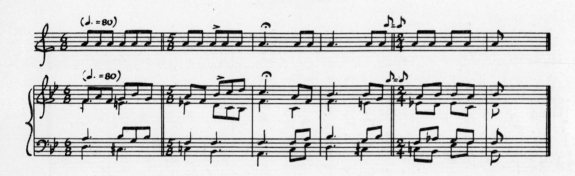

Exercise 12

Exercise 13

Exercise 14

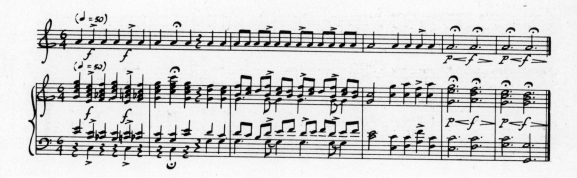

Exercise 15

Chapter XXIV

MUSICAL EXAMPLES FROM AMERICAN COMPOSITIONS

The following excerpts from American compositions have been chosen ex-
pressly for the purpose of illustrating many of the problems which have been
discussed in the foregoing pages. It is hoped that these examples may serve to
indicate the need for serious students of conducting to master technical difficulties in order that they may become more competent interpreters of our own
music.

Example 88

The Pleasure Dome of Kubla Khan - Chas. T. Griffes
(Revised orchestration of Frederick Stock)
Pub. by G. Schirmer, N.Y.

Reproduced from "The Pleasure Dome of Kubla Khan" by Charles T. Griffes
arranged by Frederick A. Stock, by permission of the copyright owners, G. Schirmer, Inc., New York.

Example 89
Excerpt from "Romantic" Symphony – Howard Hanson
Pub. by C. C. Birchard for the Eastman School
of Music, University of Rochester

The preceding examples have been chosen to show the need for an accurate rhythmic sense in manipulating simultaneously different rhythmic patterns in separate melodic lines. While the burden of execution of different rhythmic patterns superimposed one upon another must rest primarily with the players, only the basic pattern being conducted, the necessity for utmost accuracy on the part of the conductor is imperative. A classic example of the basic rhythm of six against four occurs in Wagner's Parsifal. Dr. Muck was able to help in solving the problem for his orchestra by conducting simultaneously six with his right hand and four with his left hand.

It is suggested that complete ambidexterity in tapping simultaneously two against three, three against four, and four against six, be mastered by the student.

Example 90a
Excerpt from "Pan and the Priest" - Howard Hanson
Published by C. C. Birchard for the Eastman School
of Music, University of Rochester

Example 90b
Excerpt from "Pan and the Priest" - Howard Hanson

The above examples show how the composer has given a melody, quite simple
in its first rhythmic setting, a most ingenious new rhythmic treatment. The need
for accuracy in dealing with this problem from the technical point of view is ob-
vious. The melodic line (Ex. 90a) carried by the strings must retain its essential rhythmic value while other details of the orchestration are also given due
attention.

Example 91
Excerpt from "Romantic" Symphony - Howard Hanson

Example 92
Excerpt from "Pan and the Priest" - Howard Hanson

The two preceding examples show the composer's skillful use of cross accentuation. Reference again to pp. 76-77 will recall other exercises and examples for study in connection with this particular problem of off-beat accents.

Example 93
Excerpt from "Tam-o-Shanter" - George Chadwick
Pub. by Boston Music Co.

Reproduced from "Tam-o-Shanter" by Chadwick by permission of the copyright owners, The Boston Music Company, Boston.

Example 93 will serve to show the need for adequate technique in the fermata and release, which the author has tried to stress in the foregoing pages.

Example 94
Excerpt from "Prarie", A Poem for Orchestra - Sowerby
Pub. by C. C. Birchard for the Eastman School of Music,
University of Rochester

Example 95
Excerpt from "Prarie" - Sowerby

In the above examples the problem must be solved by the giving of very accurate indications for the even continuity of the eighth note values. The tempo being too fast to beat each eighth note, the even eighth note values must be indicated by the giving of uneven four- or three-beat measures. (Refer again to p. 50)

Example 96
Excerpt from Concerto for Oboe - Irvine McHose
(Manuscript)

Example 97
Excerpt from "Three Eastern Dances" - Bernard Rogers
(Manuscript)

    Examples 96 and 97 again show the need for accurate and decisive rhythmic
changes, eighth note values remaining constant.

Chapter XXV

THE PSYCHOLOGICAL ASPECTS OF CONDUCTING

The technical side of the conductor's art must be acquired as the result of assiduous practice and training. As Scherchen puts it, (6,21)

> All training is of a technical order; and the technique of
> conducting must be learnt, as any other. When conductors try
> to learn their job from an orchestra the orchestra should re-
> fuse to play. A virtuoso instrumentalist performing works of
> art without having acquired adequate technical grounding is
> an impossibility; but an exactly analogous situation has aris-
> en in the course of all conductors' education and actual ca-
> reer even up to the present day.

In the preceding pages the attempt has been made to supply the student with material for the study of this necessary technical background.

There are still those who believe that the conductor is born and not made, that he just comes into being because he instinctively knows how. This point of view finds an amusing expression in the following quotation from Felix Mottl (5,40), who said, when he was asked how one learned to conduct, "Man steht eines Tages am Pult, und wenn mans kann, dann kann mans, und wenn man nicht kann, lernt mans überhaupt nicht mehr." The grain of truth which may be found at the bottom of the above antiquated notion probably has to do with the fact that technical knowledge is not enough; that the conductor must possess those unteachable qualities of leadership which only so few possess. Scherchen (6,4) expresses the same idea as follows:

> When the student confronts an orchestra, he must be fully
> equipped in the matter of technique. He must not be capable
> only of using with utmost accuracy the processes of his craft,
> but must know how to subordinate the orchestra's multiple per-
> sonality to his own conception of the work.

Again he states, (6,21) "The force of personality and artistic potency cannot be acquired; that much is nature's gift." This subordination of the orchestra's multiple personality to that of the conductor demands qualities and capabilities which are not so easily analyzed and which are often the despair of teachers. One can only give advice on matters of routine and the mutual relationship of the conductor to those conducted, hoping that this advice may aid in the development of some of the personal traits necessary for the conductor,--that it will prove practical and not merely a collection of platitudinous precepts.

A. SUGGESTIONS FOR REHEARSAL ROUTINE

The points listed below are the result of the author's own experience as an orchestral player under many different conductors. They are given as suggestions for rehearsal routine and naturally must be adapted to the particular situ-
ation confronting the conductor.

1. Do not talk too much in rehearsal. Music is important--not the person conducting the music.

2. Do not play over passages again and again without explaining how the performance may be improved. The spirit of a work can never develop from mere technical routine.

3. Do not destroy the personality of the artist playing a solo passage or making a solo entrance by overzealously cueing him in or by continually annoying him with overanxious watching.

4. Avoid sarcastic personal remarks tending to belittle a player in the eyes of his colleagues. It is best to dismiss lazy or troublesome players needing this kind of discipline.

5. Do not always explain your intentions in abstract terms. Explain what you want so that musicians can understand how to carry out your desires in terms of the technique of their instruments or voices. While subtleties in the mental conceptions of musical expression can sometimes find expression in imaginative comparisons, this type of rehearsal routine can easily be carried too far.

6. Do not demand effects which certain instruments by their very nature or technical limitations are unable to give. For instance, do not expect to obtain a fortissimo from strings in a very fast spiccato passage.

7. Do not become too emotional during rehearsal. Continuous emotional exuberance usually elicits bored amusement. Controlled emotion is more likely to find its outlet in the music.

8. One great contemporary conductor often greatly exaggerates slowness of tempo, agogic accent, and other nuances during rehearsal, much to the distaste of many musicians. Through this practice, however, the nuances impress themselves on the players and are usually given the right value at the performance. This procedure cannot be recommended except for the working out slowly of passages of great technical difficulty. It is usually best to rehearse at the performance tempo, as only then can the proper musical values be established.

9. Nothing is more irritating to string players than to have bowing continually changed. The conductor should make sure that his concertmaster has all bowings determined correctly and marked before rehearsal.

10. Do not tap continually on the music stand. It is annoying and unnecessary if proper discipline is maintained.

11. If something goes wrong in the orchestra, the inexperienced conductor should form the habit of looking first to himself to see if his own shortcomings were in any way responsible. The conductor who continually blames his own shortcomings on the orchestra is detestable.

B. ON CONDUCTING FROM MEMORY

The conductor who conducts from memory should be very sure that he really knows his music in every note and mark with photographic exactitude. The orchestra can never be fooled on this point and has no liking for the man calling himself conductor who memorizes seventy-two bars in four and then knows he must change to three. The questionable practice of conducting from memory, probably started by some of our greatest conductors, has had a very insidious effect on many who feel that they must imitate them, but who seldom can. No better opinion regarding conducting from memory has been voiced than that of Weingartner, who says, (9,42)

This (conducting from memory) makes a great impression on the
audience, but I do not place too high a value on it. In my
opinion a conductor may really know a work by heart and yet
fear that his memory may play him a trick, either through par-
donable excitement or some other disturbing influence. In such
cases it is always better to use the score; the audience is
there to enjoy the work, not to admire the memory of the conductor. I recommend doing without the score only when knowledge of it is combined with such a mastery of oneself that
reference to it is more a hindrance than a help, and the conductor, though he may read a page now and then, yet feels that
to use the score throughout the whole work would be putting a
needless fetter on himself. It is all a purely personal matter,
however, that has nothing to do with the perfection of the performance. If the conductor is so dependent on the score that
he can never take his eyes from it to look at the players, he
is of course a mere time-beater, a bungler, with no pretension
to the title of artist. Conducting from memory, however, that
makes a parade of virtuosity is also inartistic, since it di-
verts attention from the work to the conductor. Now and then
we see a conductor put a score on the stand although he conducts from memory, his object being not to attract too much at-
tention--a proceeding that I think commendable. But I hold
that it is entirely the conductor's own concern whether he will
use the score or not. A good performance from the score has
value; a bad one done from memory has none.

As stated before, precepts concerning the conductor's conduct in rehearsal
can never make him a forceful leader, but it is hoped that the advice given above
may serve to help somewhat in the building of that intangible characteristic
called forceful personality and leadership, through the development of tact and
sound judgment.

Although quoted many times in textbooks on conducting, no more excellent
summing up of the situation can be offered than the following excerpt from Weingartner (9,56).

More and more I have come to think that what decides the worth
of conducting is the degree of suggestive power that the conductor can exercise over the performers. At the rehearsals he
is mostly nothing more than a work-man, who schools the men
under him so conscientiously and precisely that each of them
knows his place and what he has to do there; he first becomes
an artist when the moment comes for the production of the work.
Not even the most assiduous rehearsing, so necessary a prereq-
uisite as this is, can so stimulate the capacities of the
players as the force of imagination of the conductor. It is
not the transference of his personal will, but the mysterious
act of creation that called the work itself into being which
takes place again in him, and, transcending the narrow limits
of reproduction, he becomes a new-creator, a self-creator.
The more, however, his personality disappears so as to get
quite behind the personality that created the work,--to iden-
tify itself, indeed, with this--the greater will his performance be.

Chapter XXVI

CONCLUSION

Any concluding remarks can only serve to emphasize the fact that perfection in the technical elements of conducting can never transform a poor musician into a good conductor. Nor can such a course of study as outlined in the preceding chapters ever substitute adequately for actual experience, not only in conducting, but in being competently conducted.

Today young musicians find their musical experience in school orchestras, bands, and choruses, whereas twenty-five years ago the professional theater orchestra gave the competent young player the first taste of the musical experience which later led the most talented into the ranks of our symphony orchestras. While it is true today that many of our high school orchestras play better than the old theater orchestras did, it is also a regrettable fact that even in professional music schools programs are rehearsed and rehearsed to their own standards of perfection at the expense of sight-reading experience and a wider knowledge of musical literature. In the high school field, which is still largely dominated by the contest idea, a few pieces of music, usually selected by some outside group, entirely absorb the attention of the musical groups over long periods of time. This situation does not help the aspiring young musician to get the necessary background for conducting.

Many good conductors of today had to learn the many details of their profession by experience, often at the expense of the orchestra which taught them. I have tried in the preceding chapters to supply some of the needed information about the details of conducting which many older musicians may have acquired through experience.

The knowledge of the capabilities and the peculiarities of the various instruments and their transpositions, of score reading, of voice and choral training, to say nothing of musicianship and interpretational ability, cannot be treated in this book, but the author does not wish to leave the impression that he believes that the mere mechanics of gesture are more important than the other prerequisites for conducting. The great leader of men and the great musician, even though a poor technician, is preferable to a good technician who is a poor musician or devoid of other necessary knowledge.

It is hoped that many who are innately endowed with the musical gifts and the personal qualifications necessary to become conductors will find help in the foregoing pages.

THE END

BIBLIOGRAPHY

1. Berlioz, Hector. <u>The Orchestral Conductor, Theory of His Art</u>. New York: Carl Fischer, 1902.

2. Boult, Adrian C. <u>A Handbook on the Technique of Conducting</u>. London: Goodwin & Tabb, Ltd.

3. Earhart, Will. <u>The Eloquent Baton</u>. New York: M. Witmark & Sons, 1931.

4. Gehrkens, Karl Wilson. <u>Essentials in Conducting</u>. Boston: Oliver Ditson Co., 1919.

5. Kendrie, Frank Estes. <u>Handbook on Conducting and Orchestral Routine</u>. New York: H. W. Gray Co., 1930.

6. Scherchen, Herman. <u>Handbook of Conducting</u>. English translation by M. D. Calvocoressi. London: Oxford University Press, 1933.

7. Stoessel, Albert. <u>The Technique of the Baton</u>. New York: Carl Fischer, 1920.

8. Wagner, Richard. <u>On Conducting</u>. English translation by Edward Dannreuther. London: Wm. Reeves, 1897.

9. Weingartner, Felix. <u>On Conducting</u>. English translation by Ernest Newman. New York: E. F. Kalmus, Inc.

7